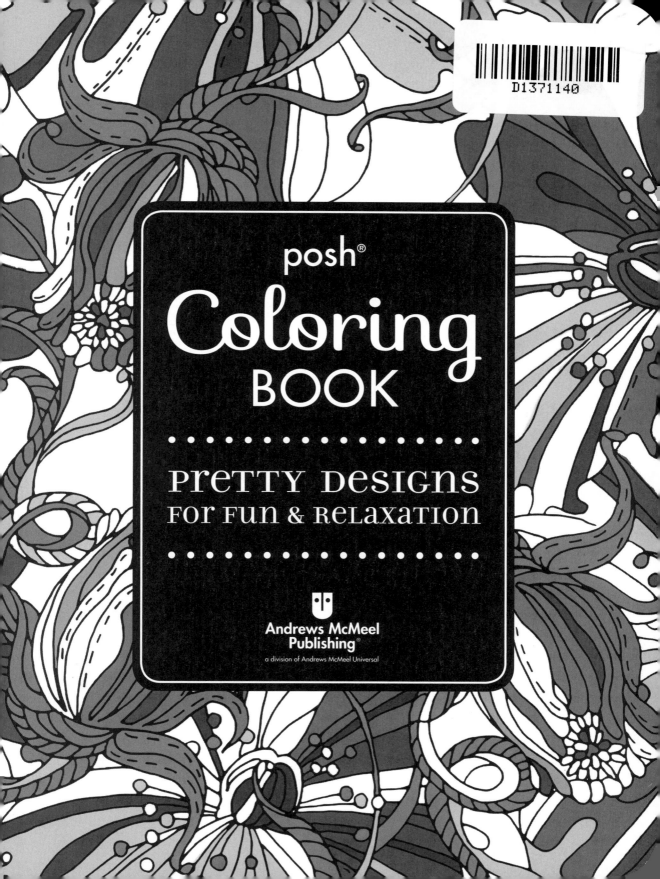

posh®

Coloring
BOOK

· · · · · · · · · · · · · · · · · · ·

PRETTY DESIGNS
FOR FUN & RELAXATION

· · · · · · · · · · · · · · · · · · ·

Andrews McMeel
Publishing®
a division of Andrews McMeel Universal

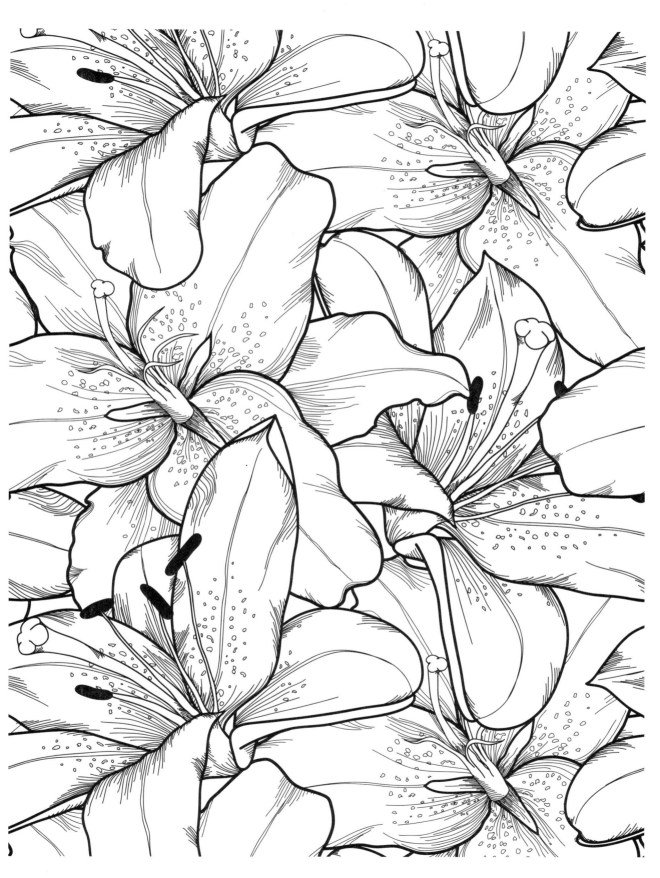

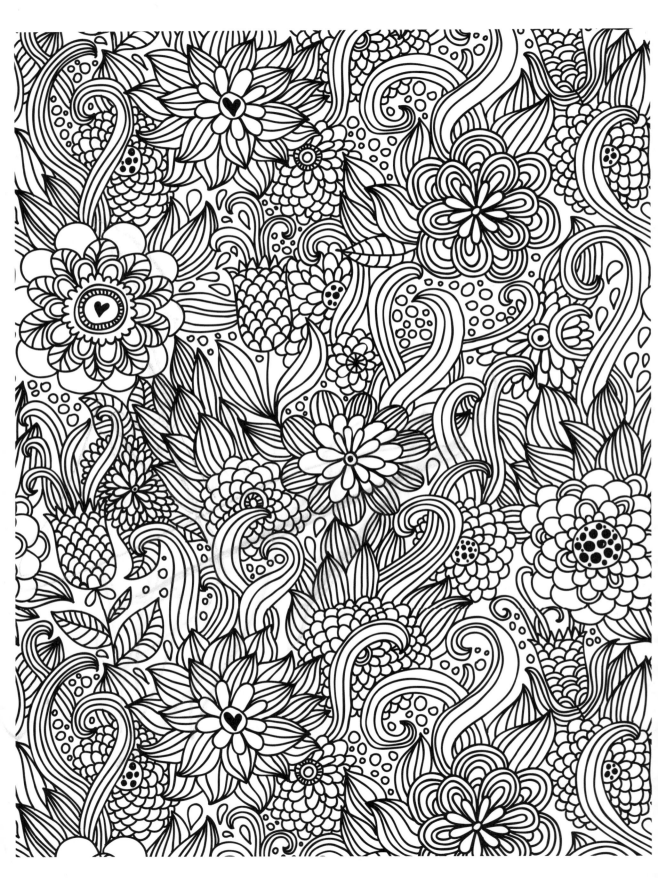

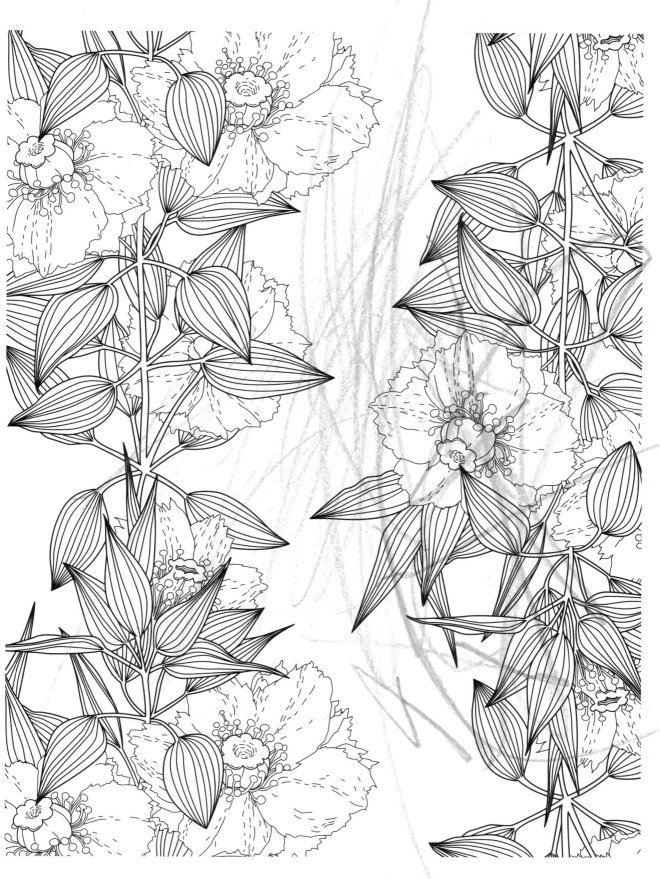

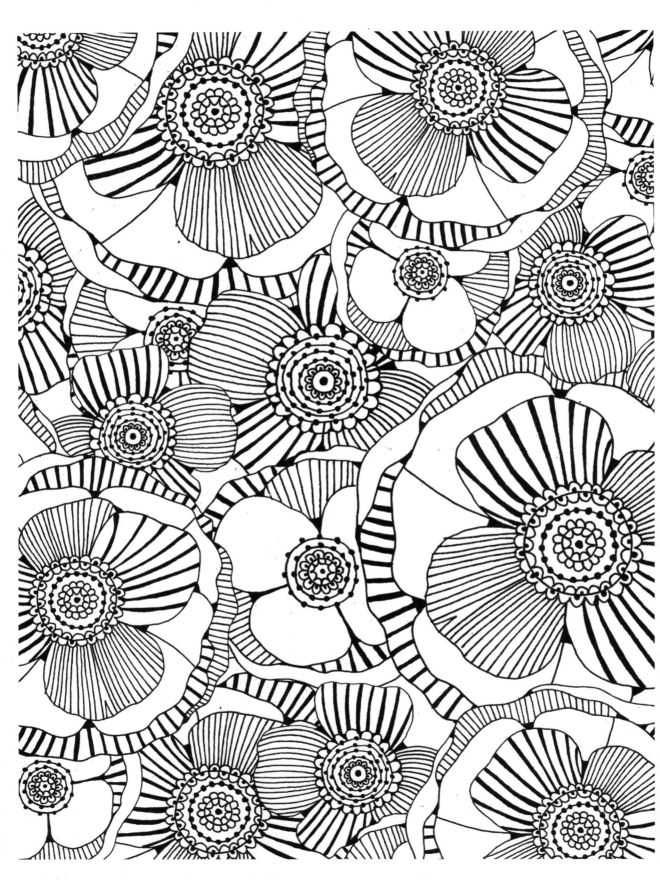

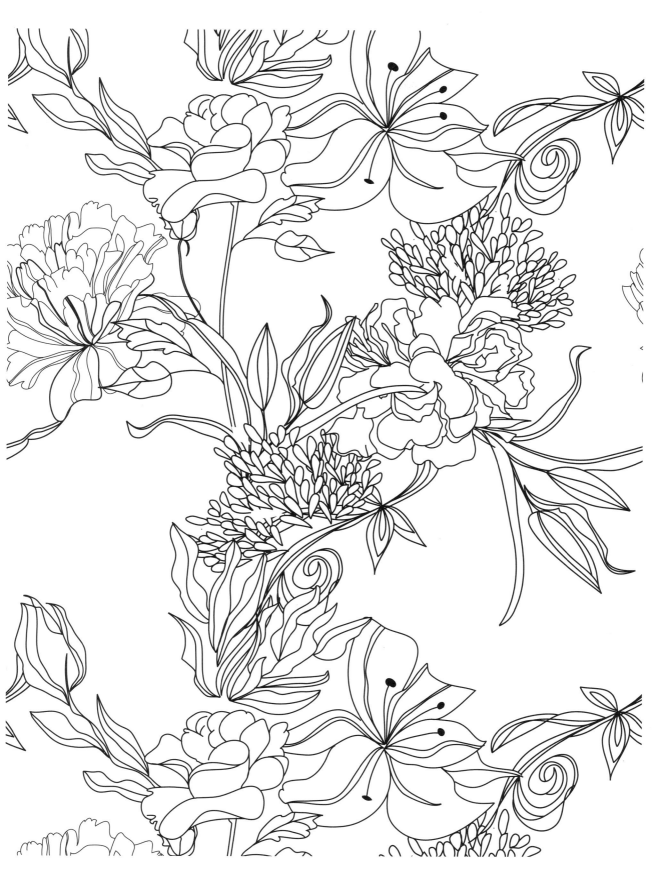

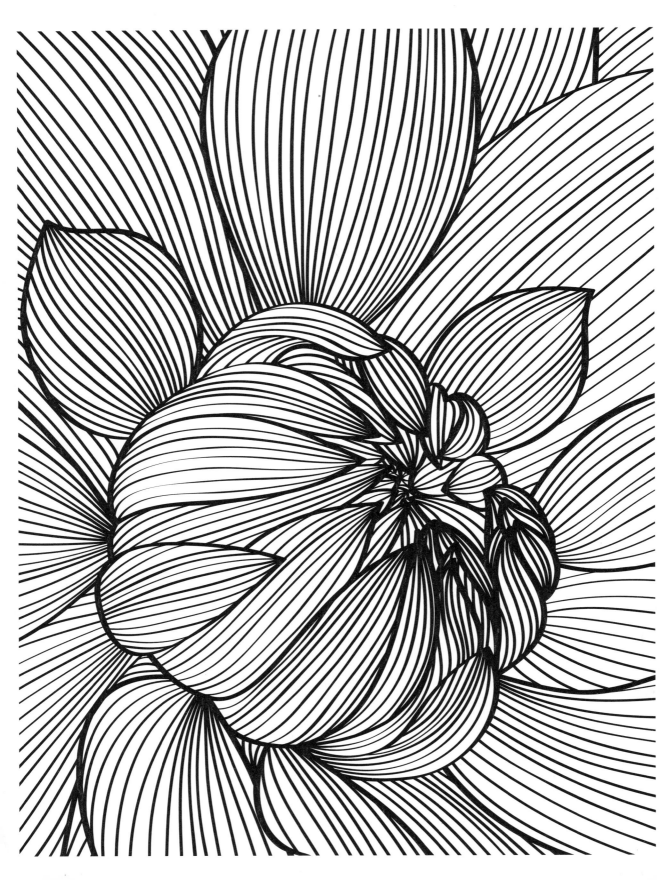

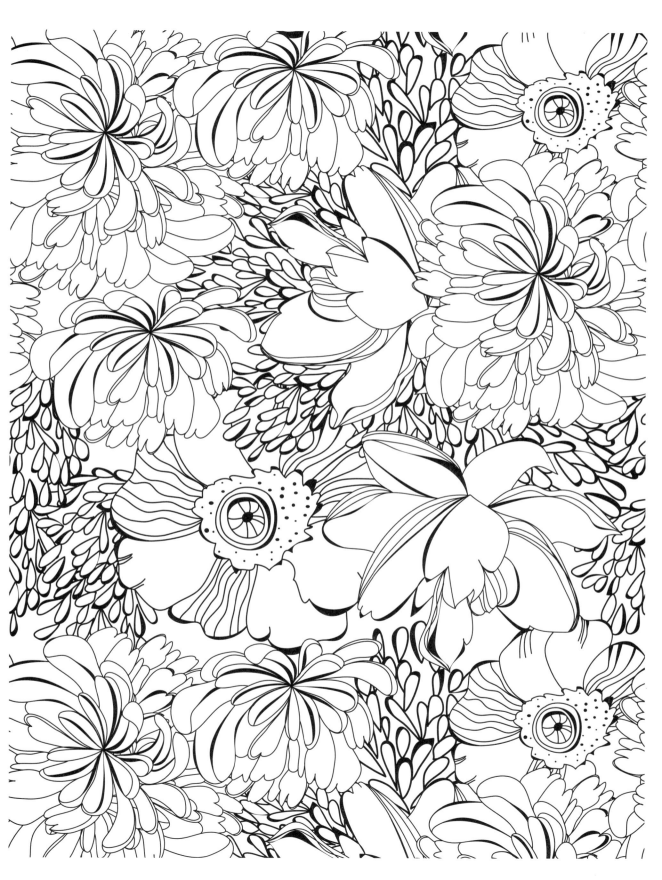

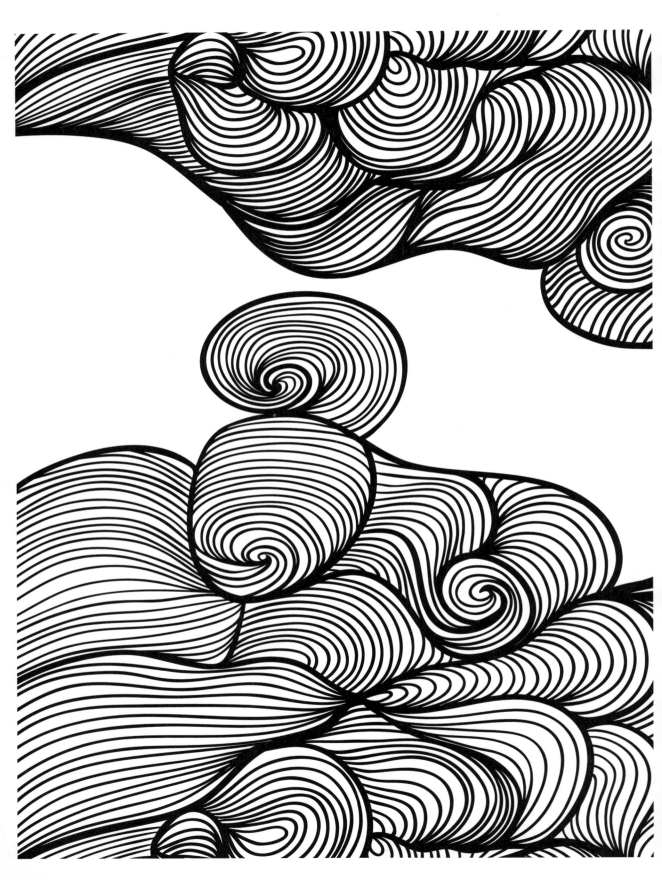

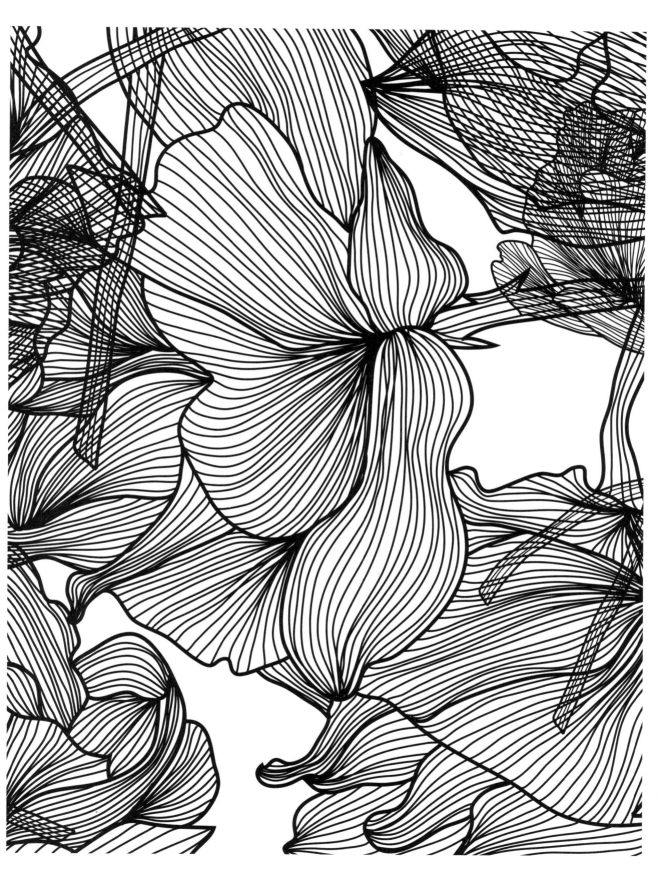

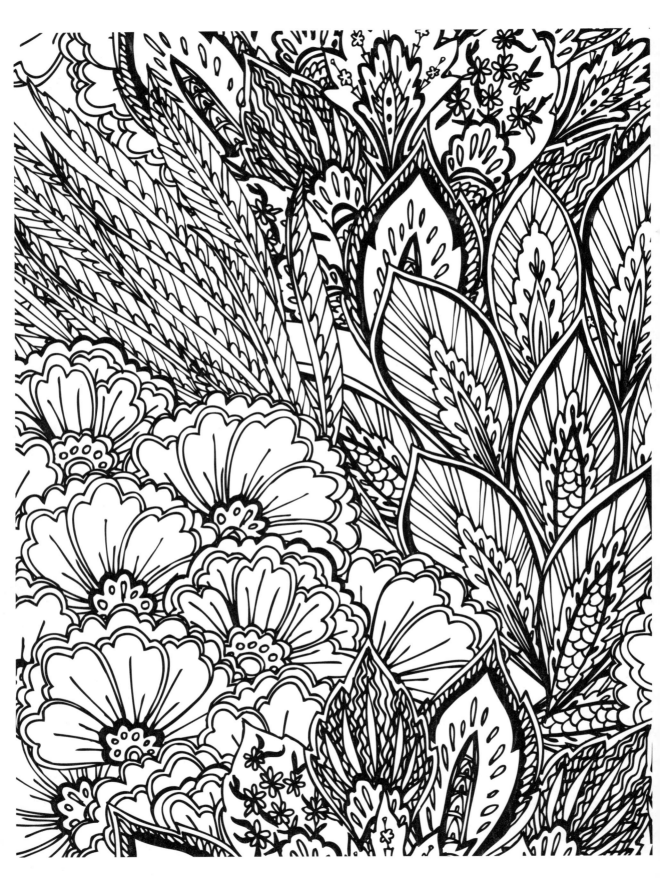

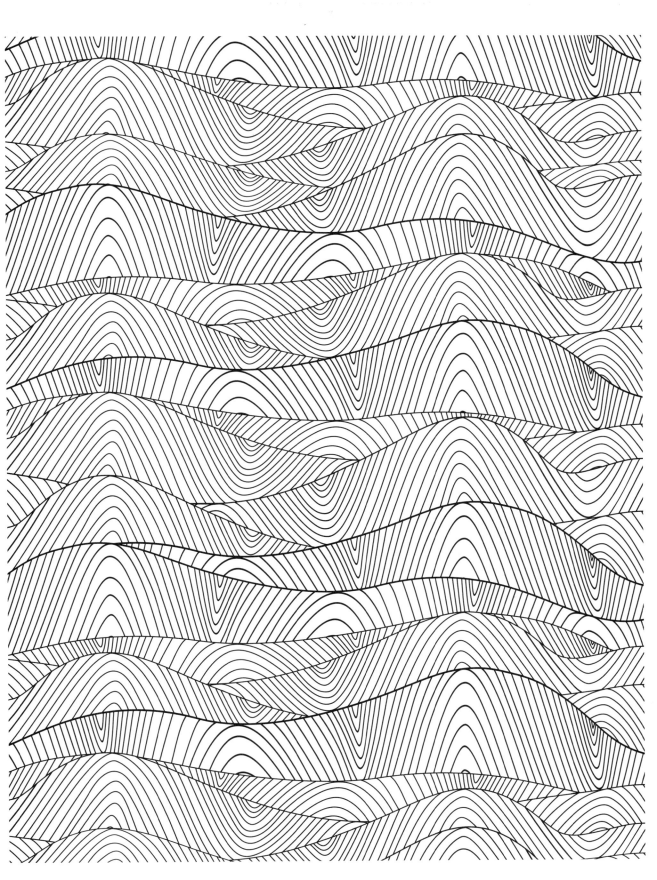

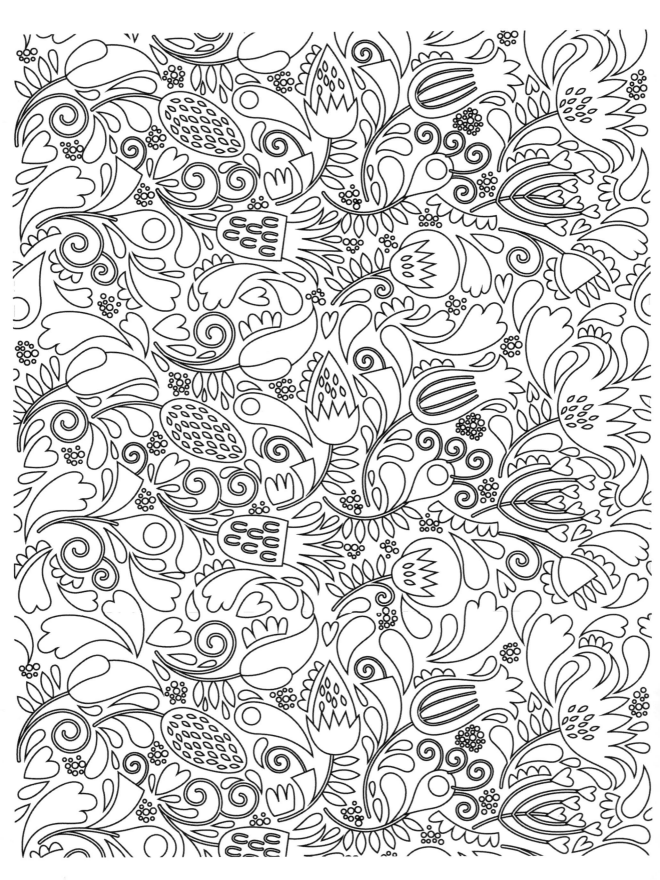

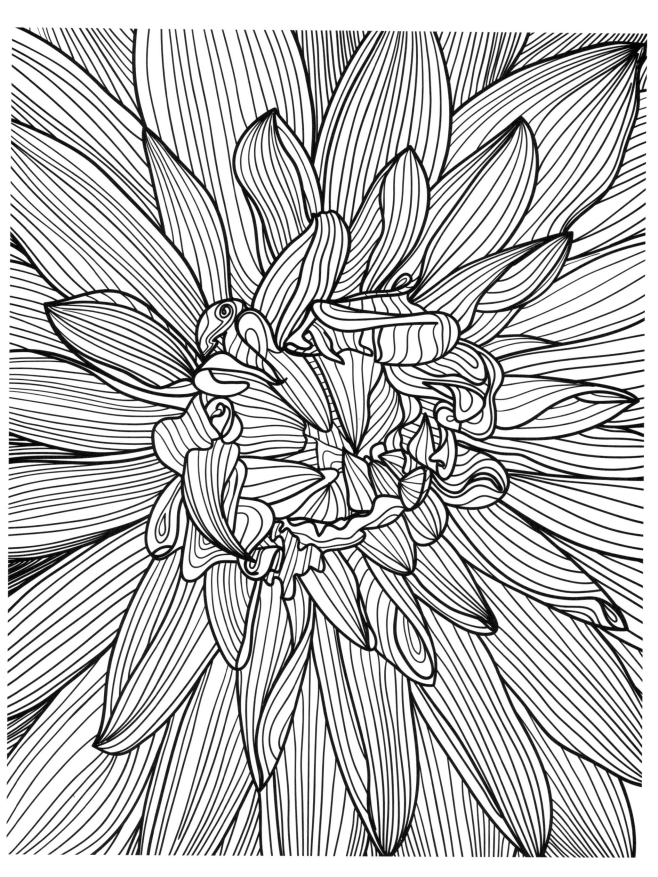

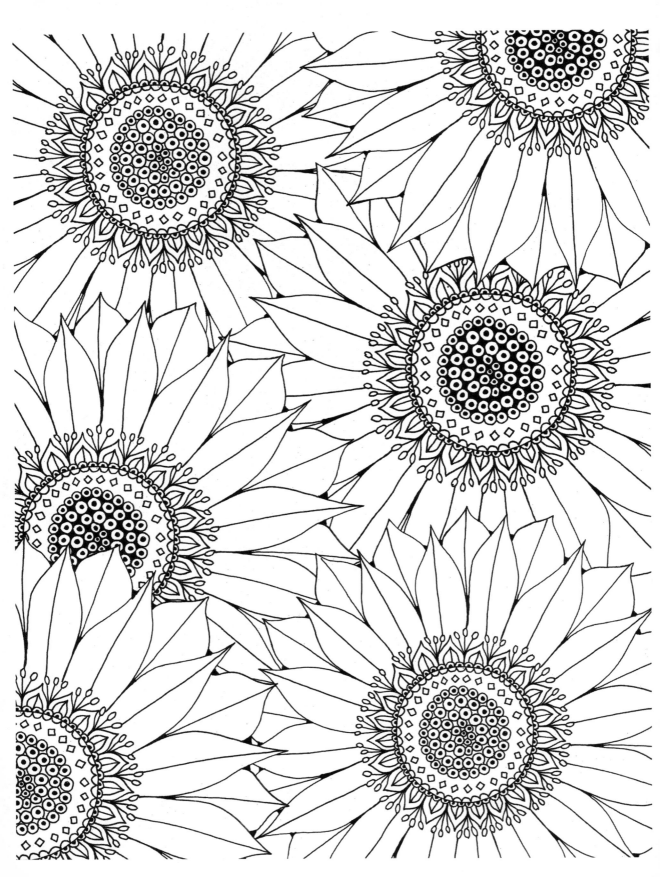

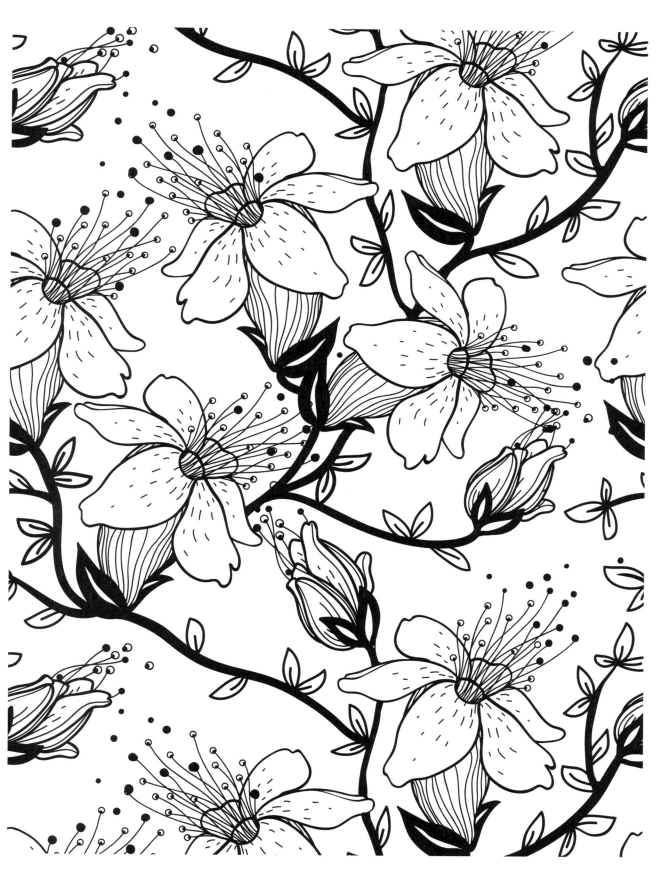

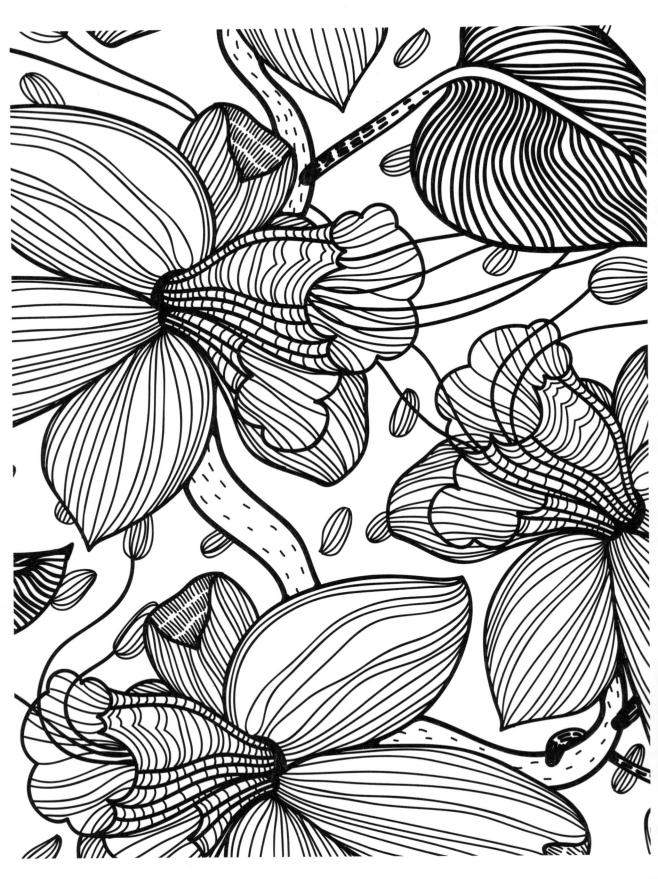

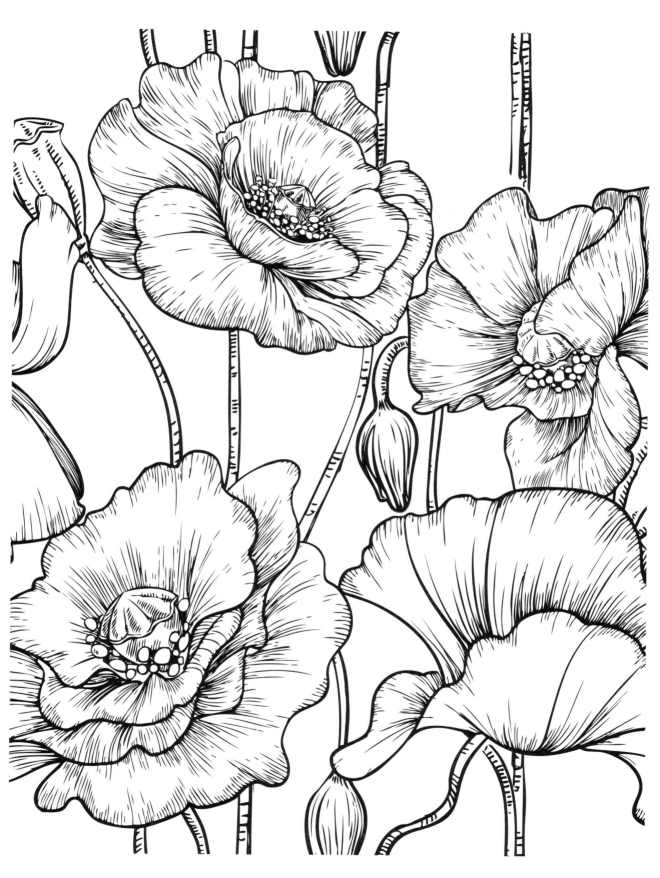

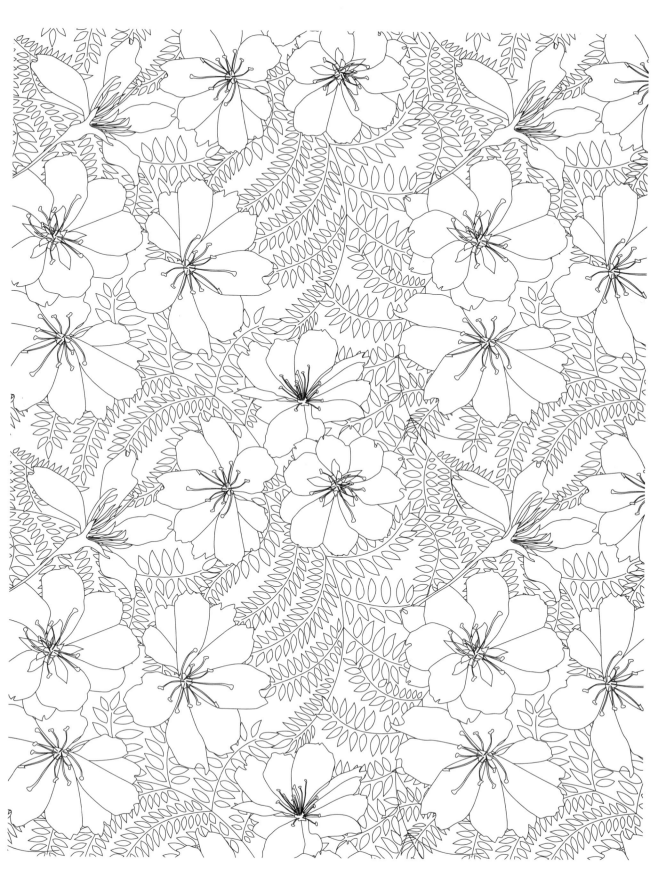

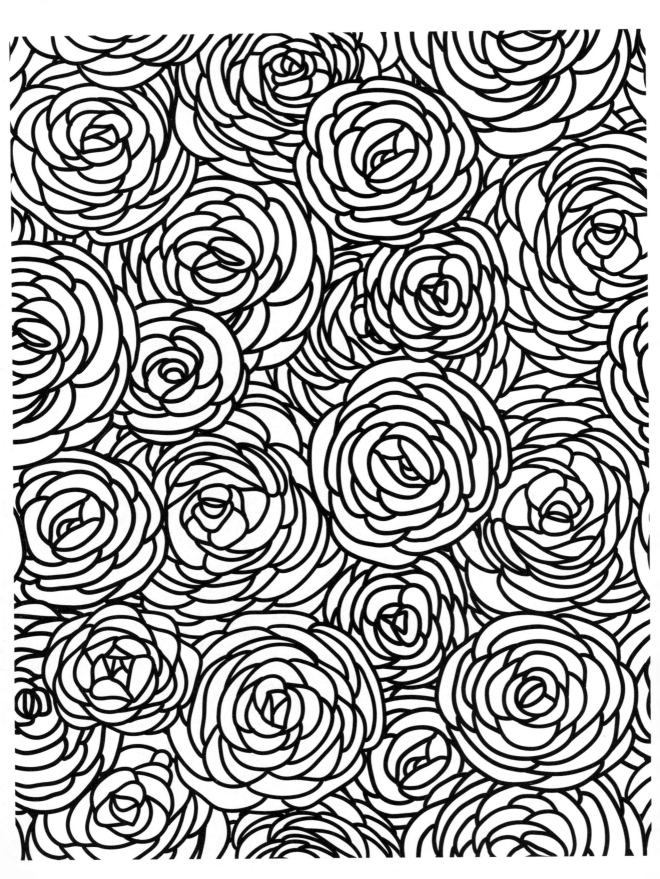

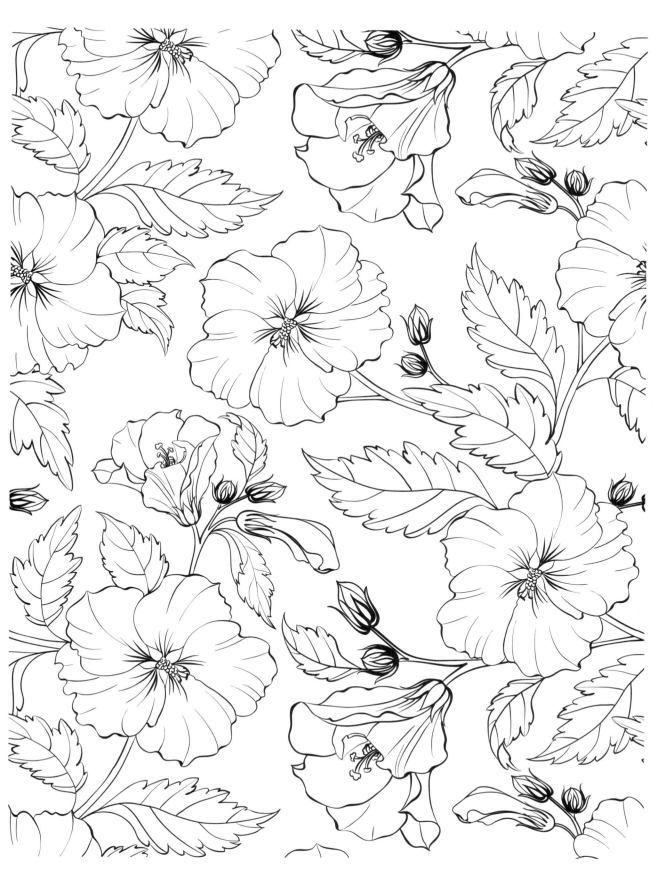

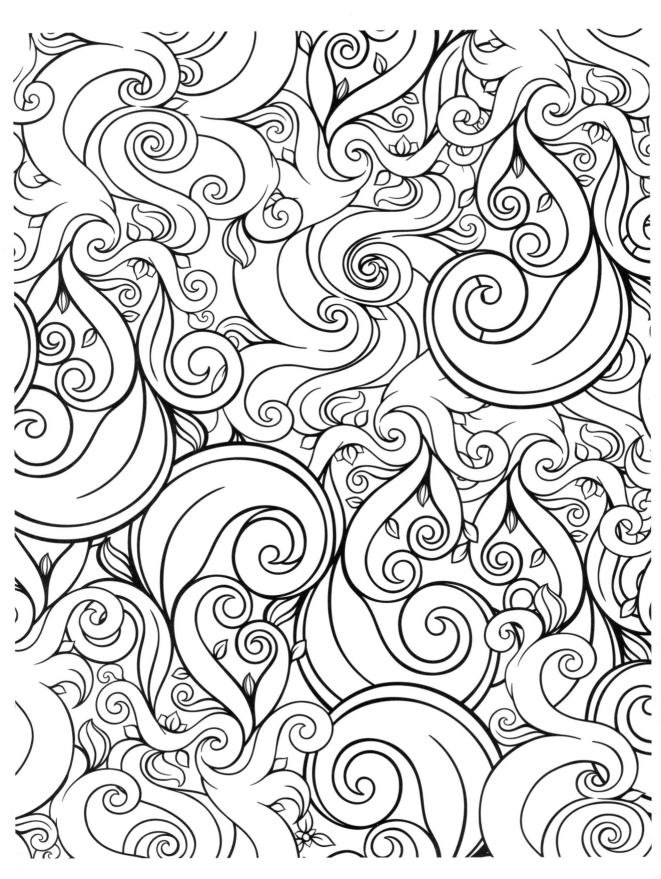

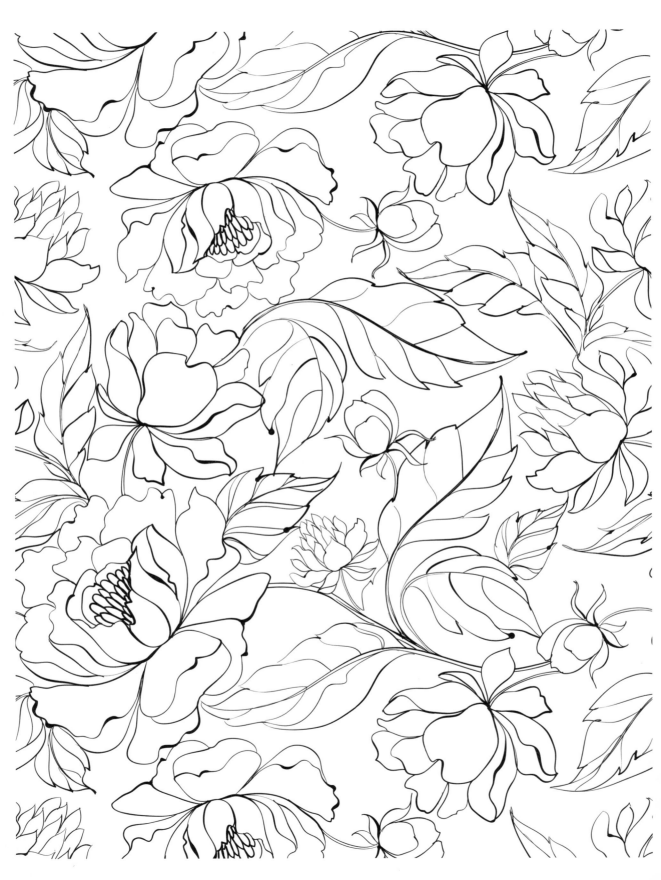

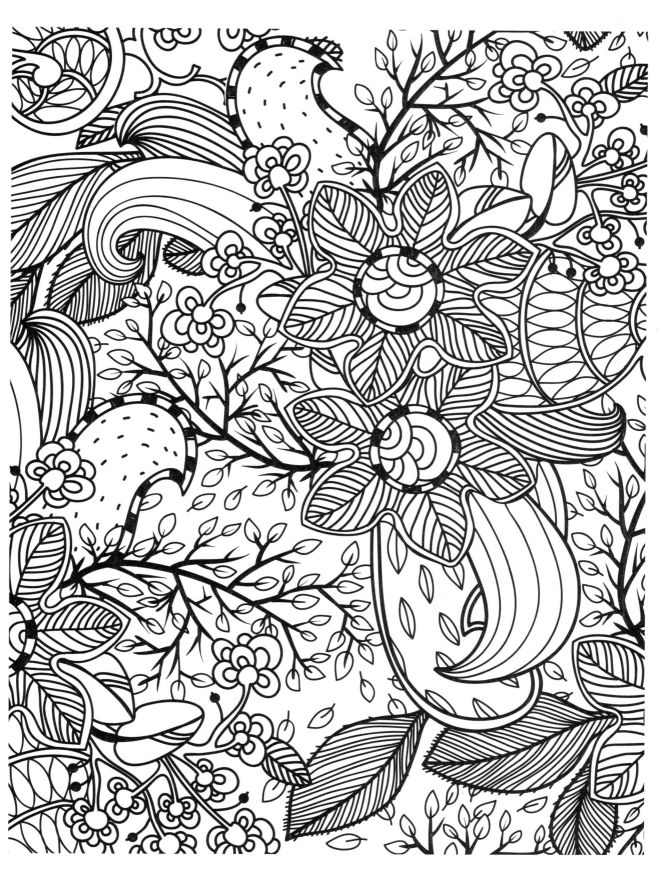

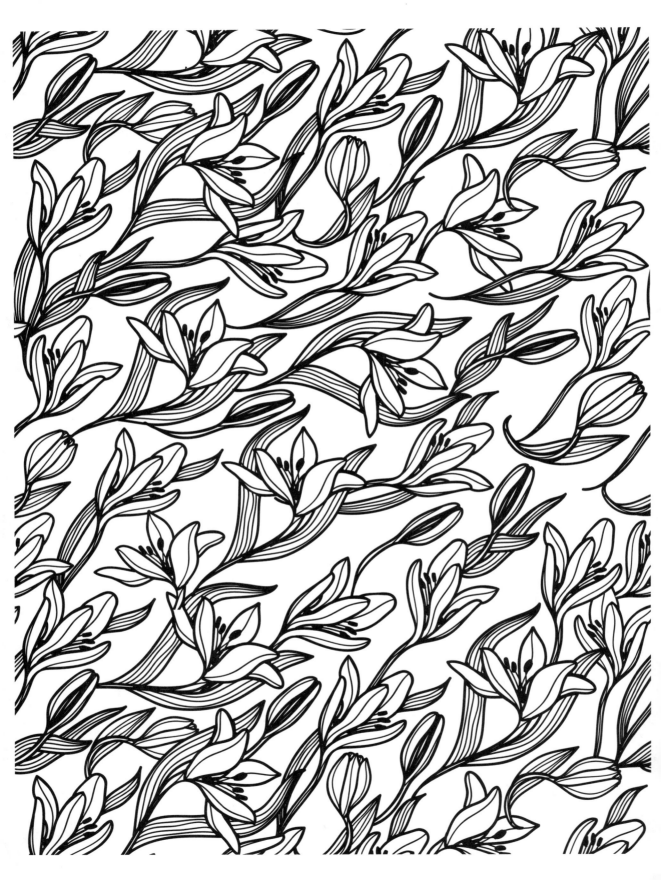

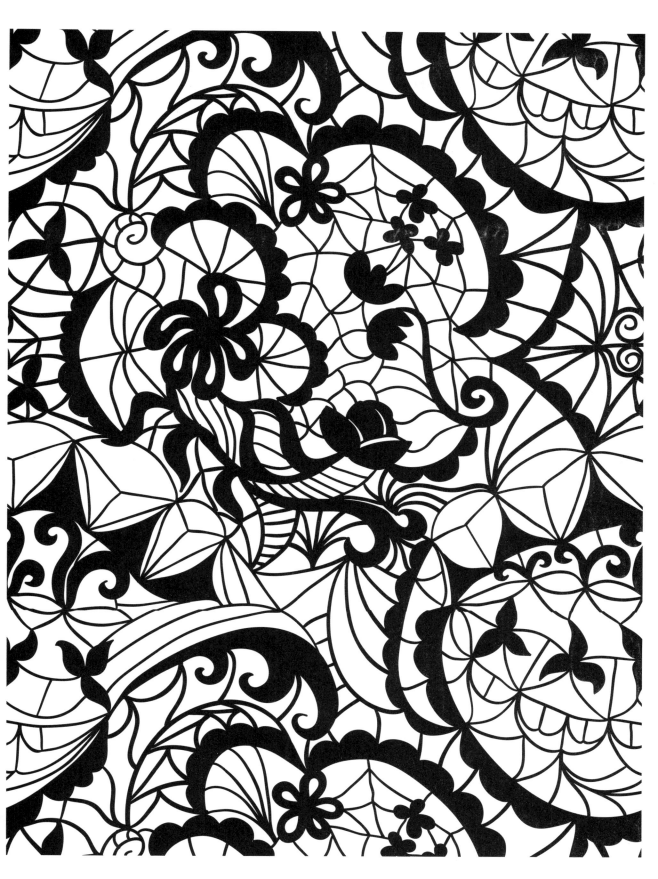

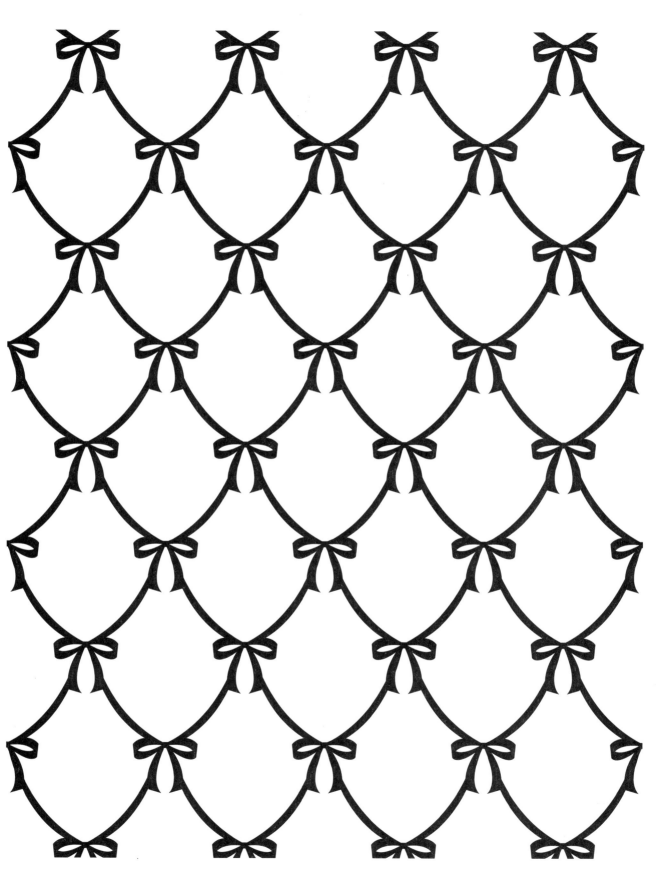

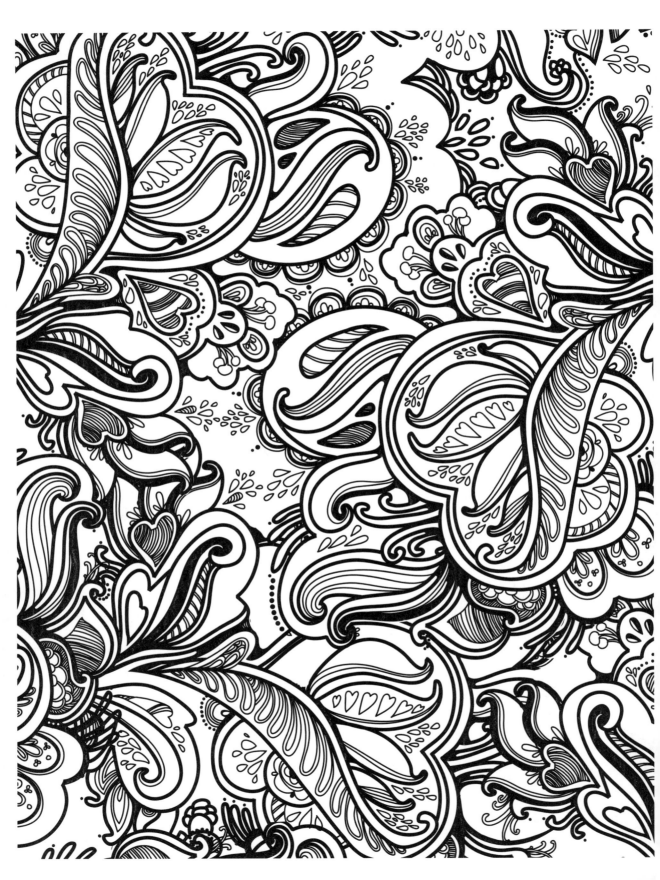

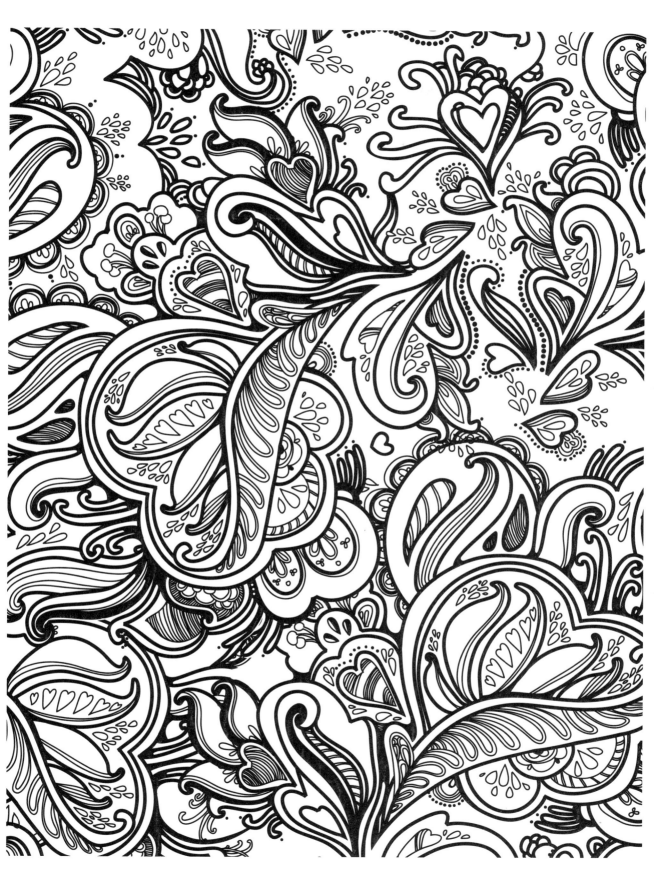

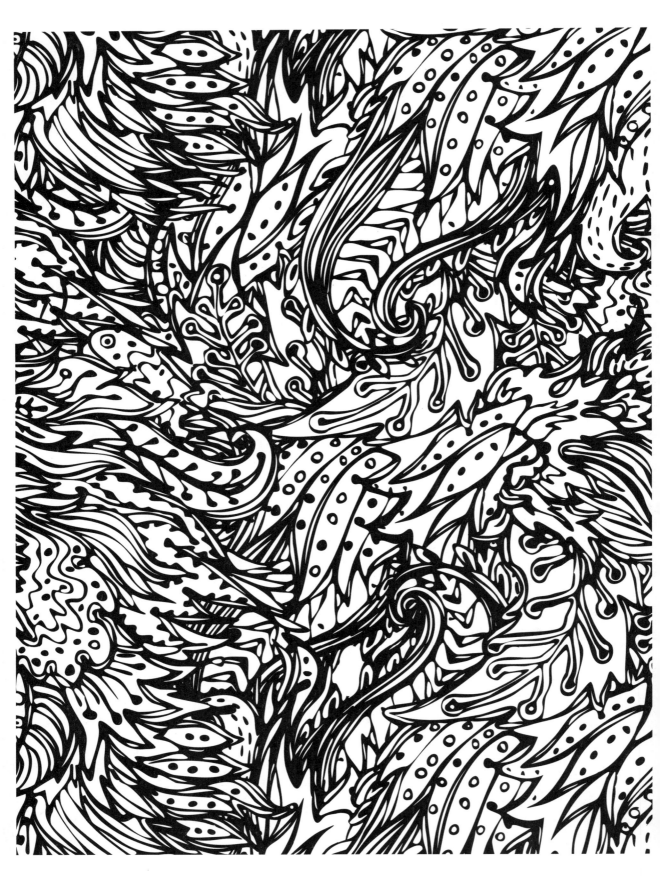

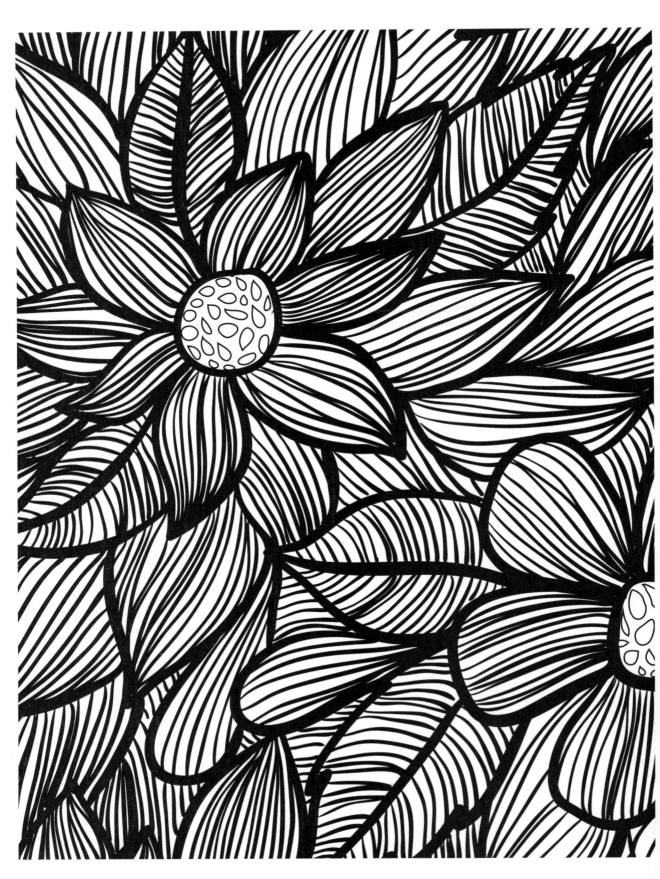

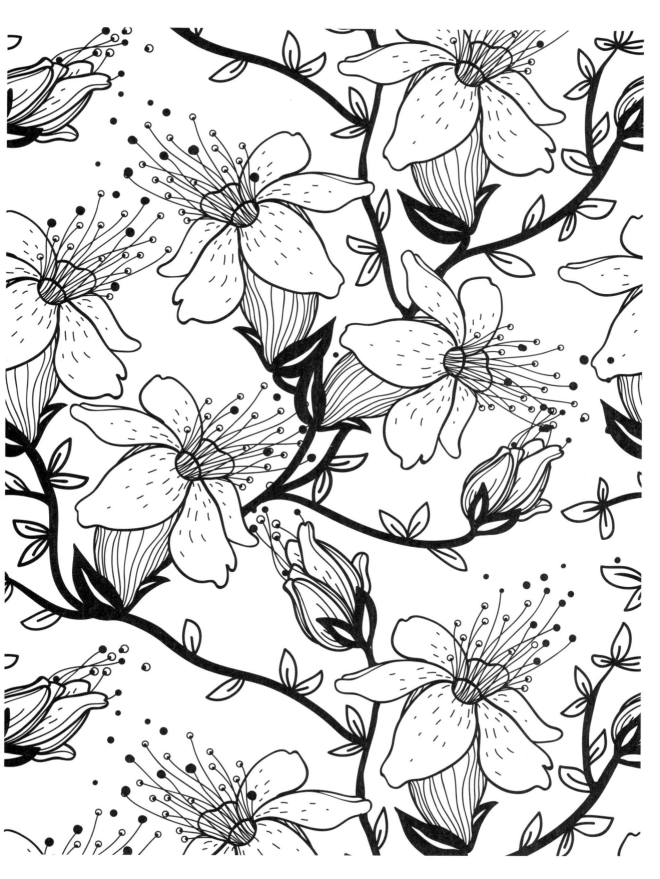

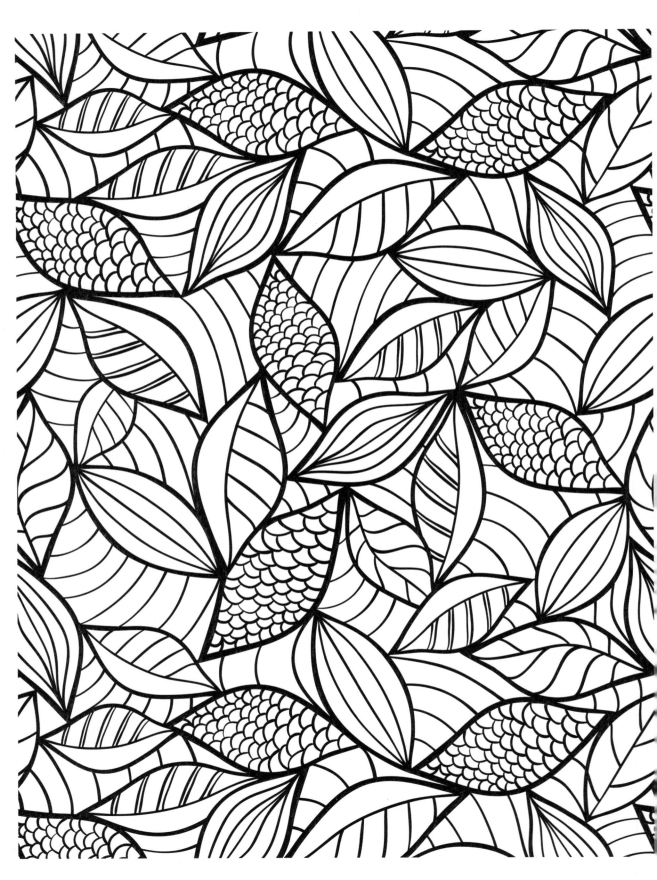

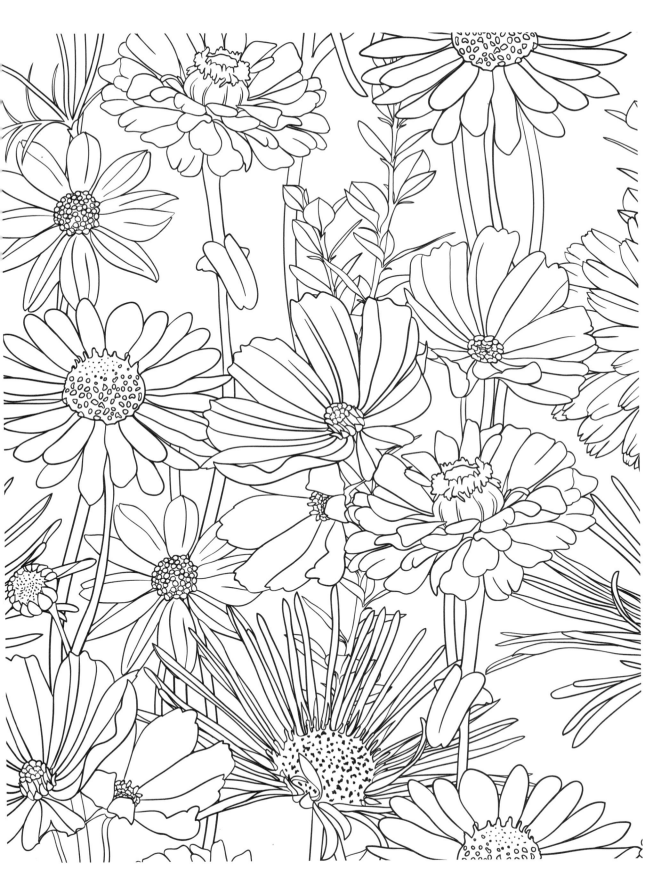

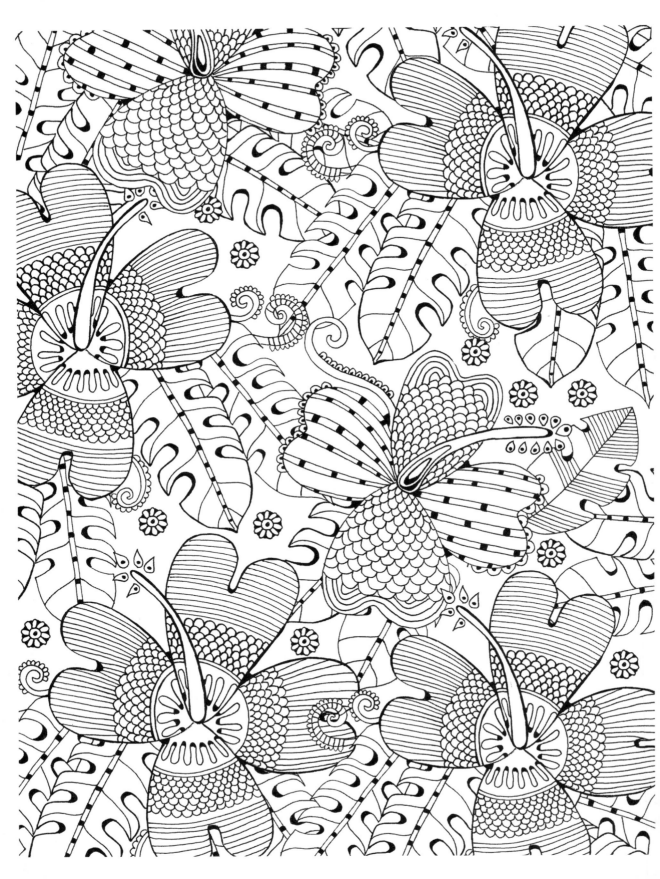

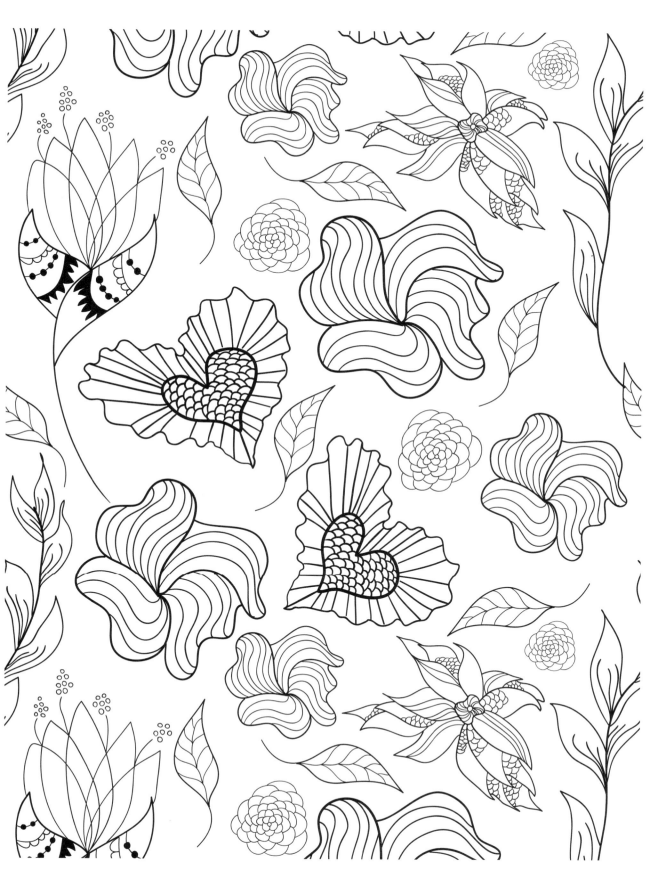

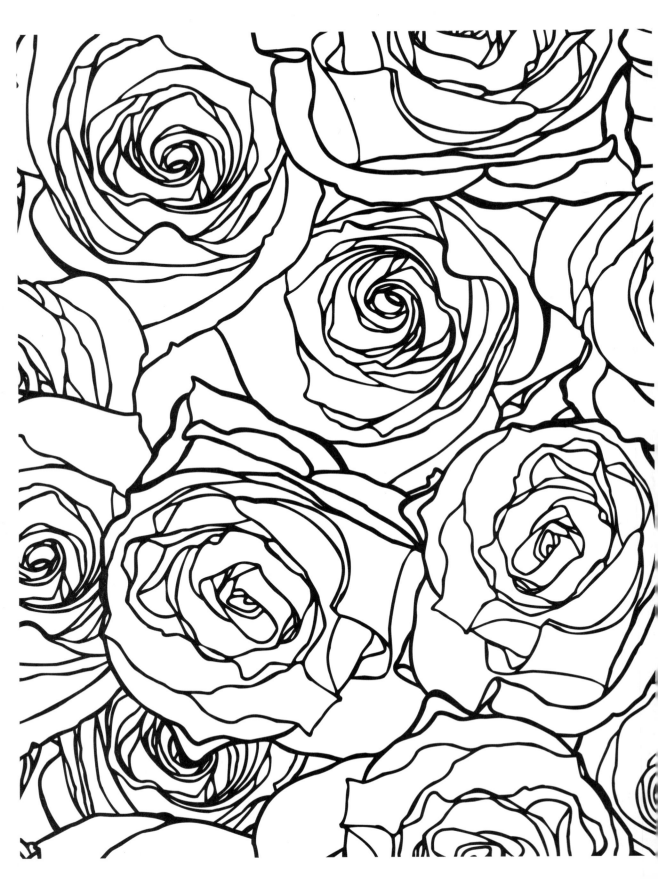

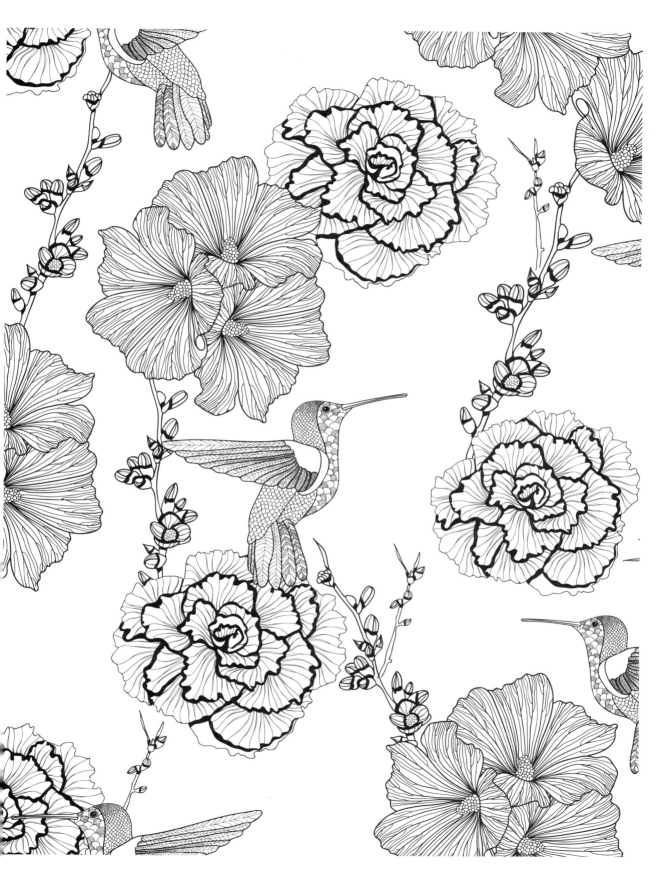

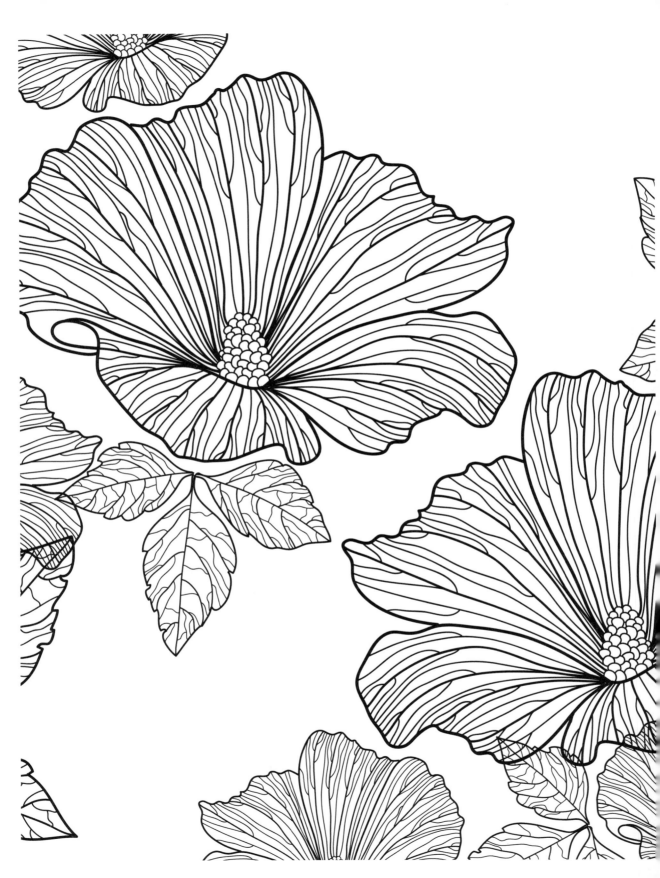

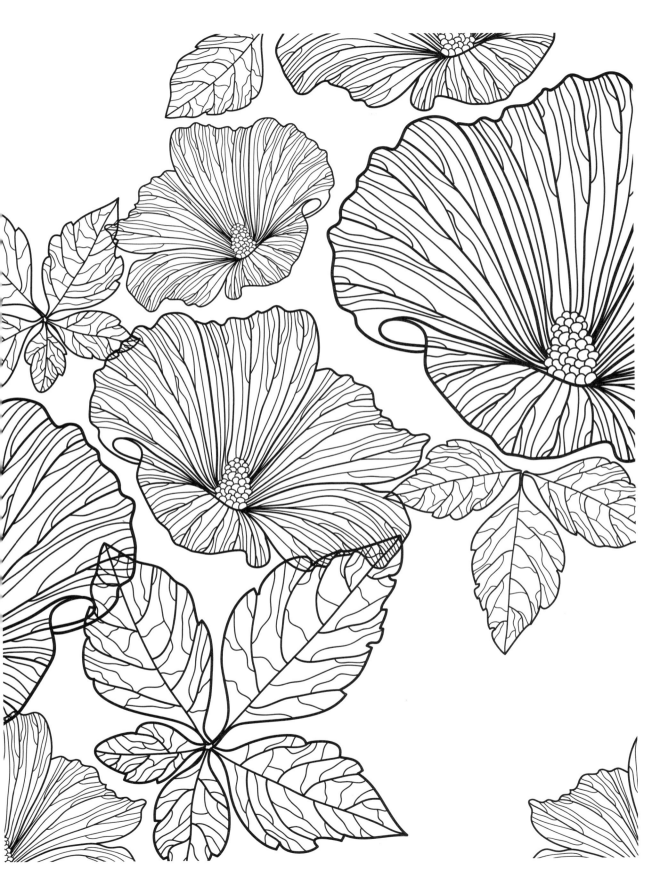

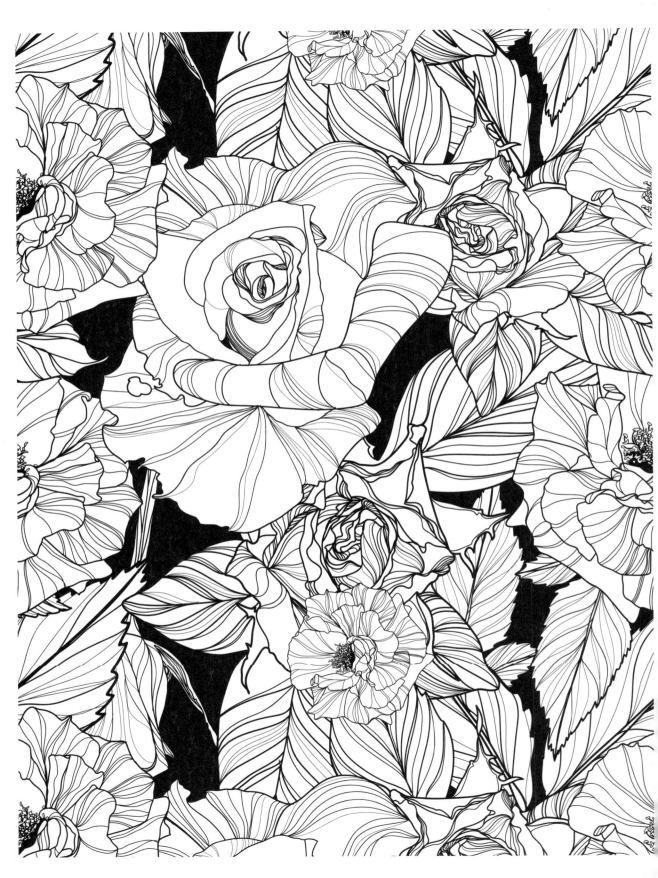

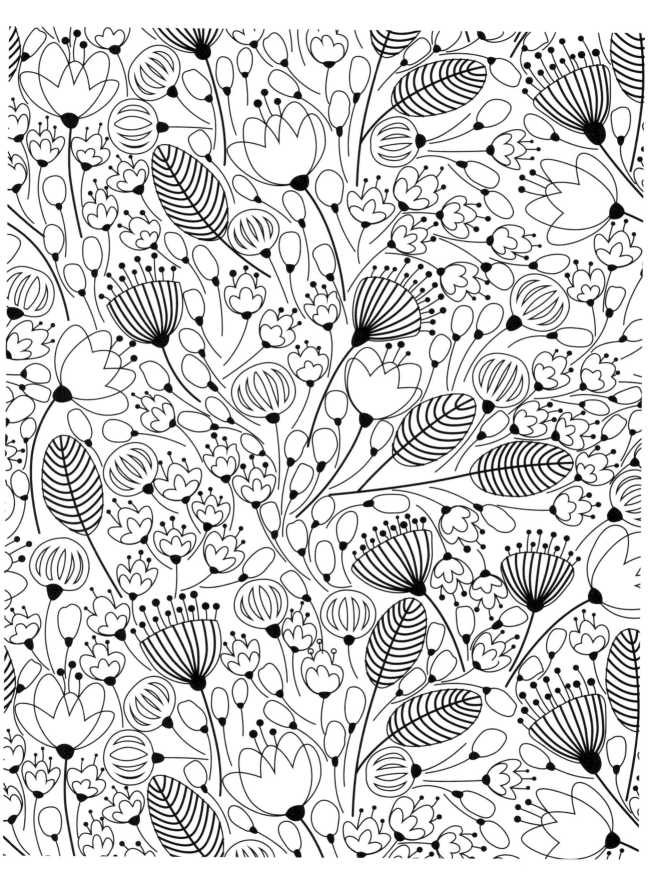

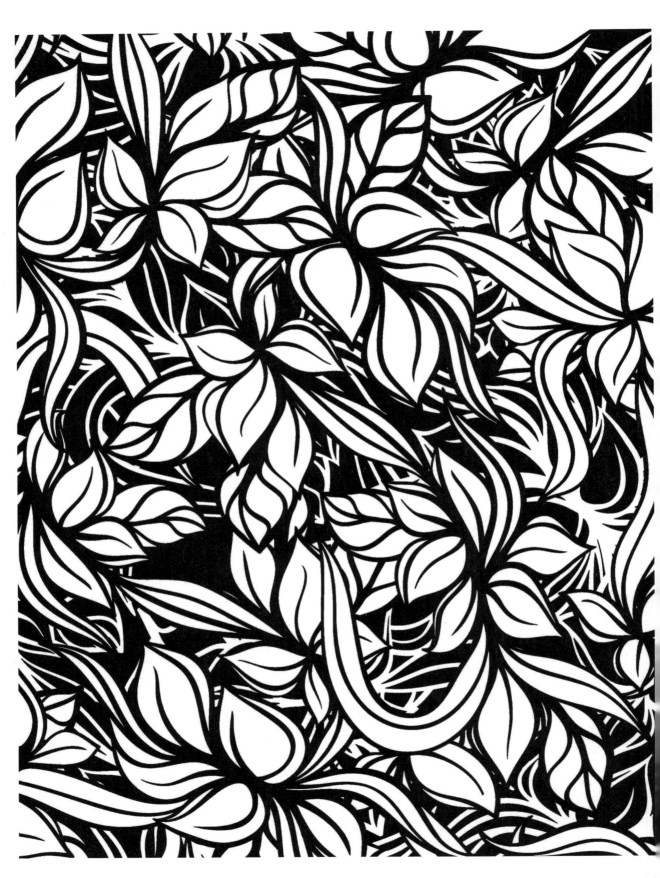

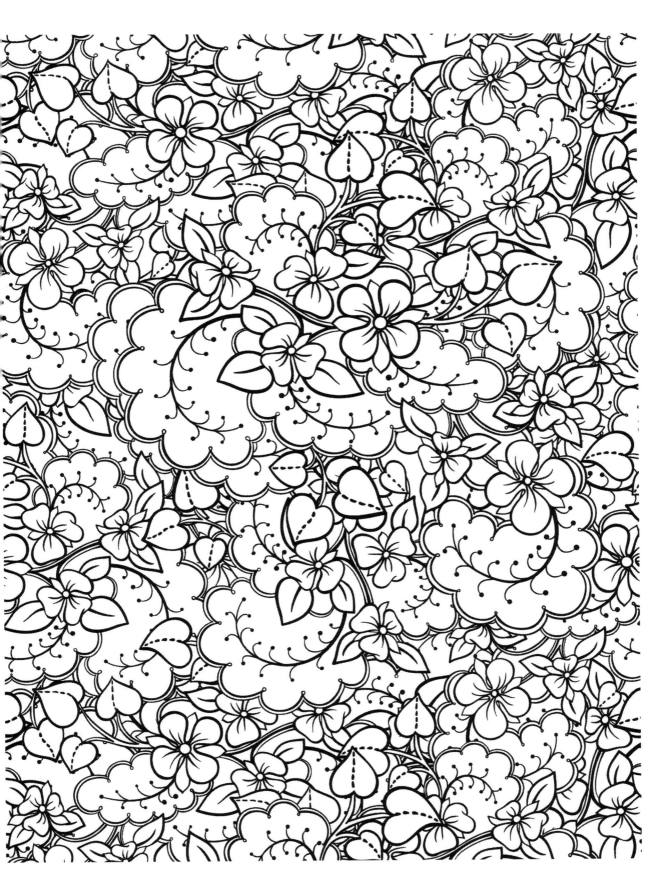

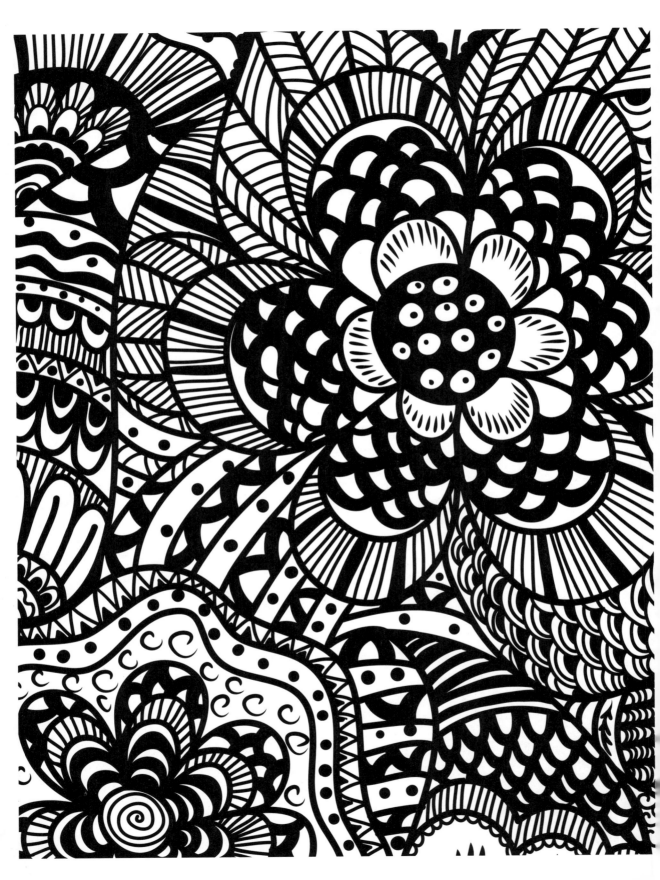

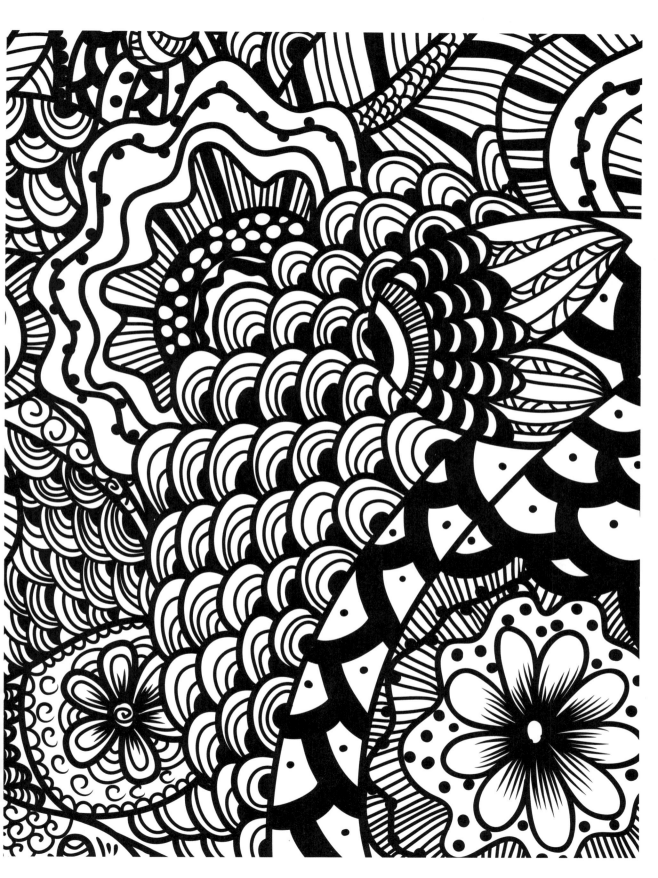

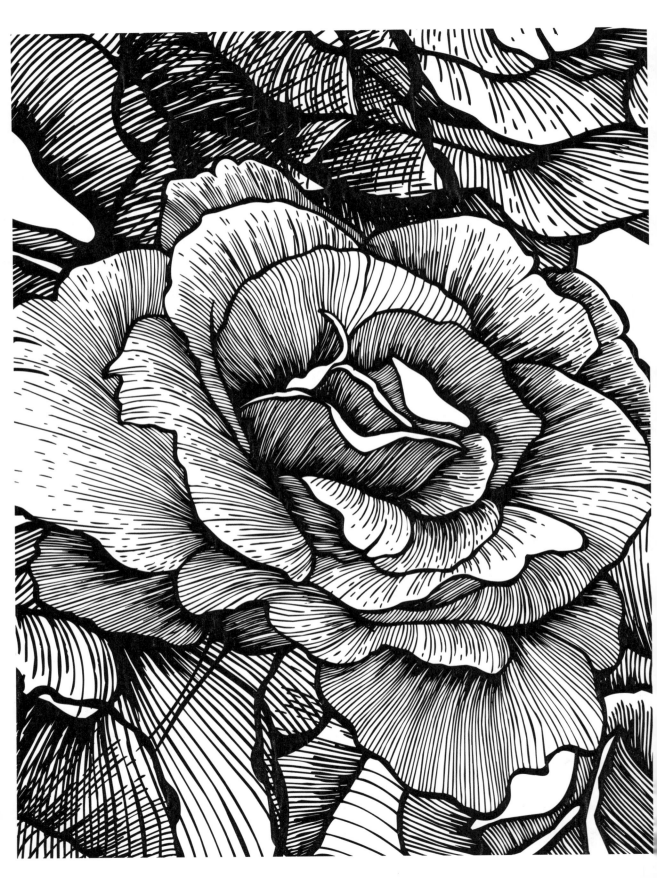

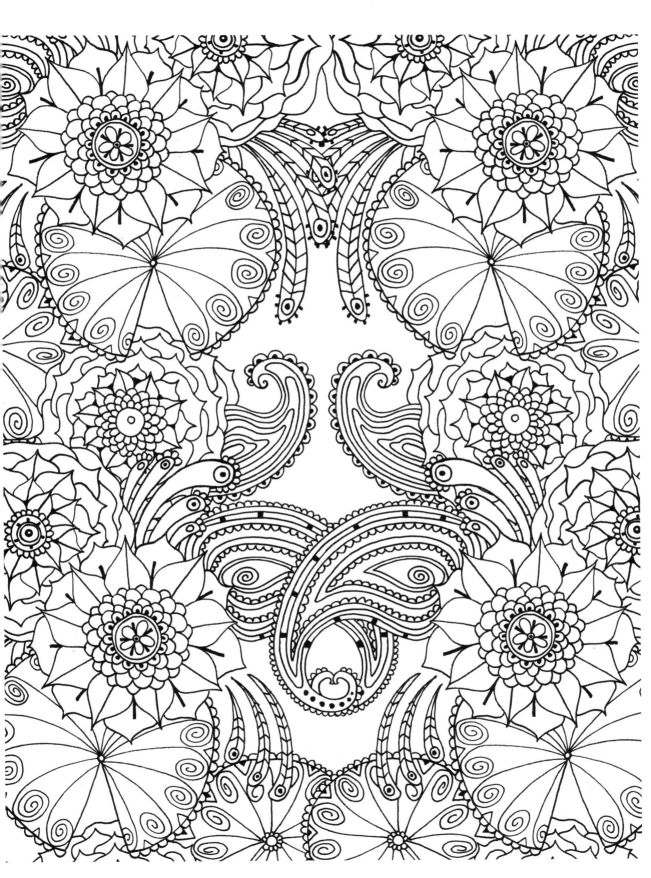

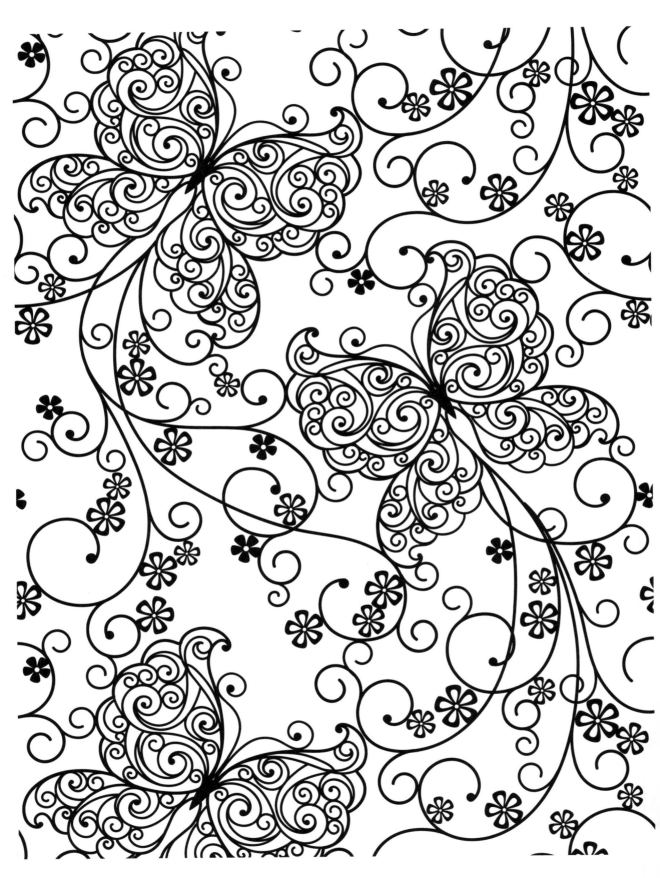

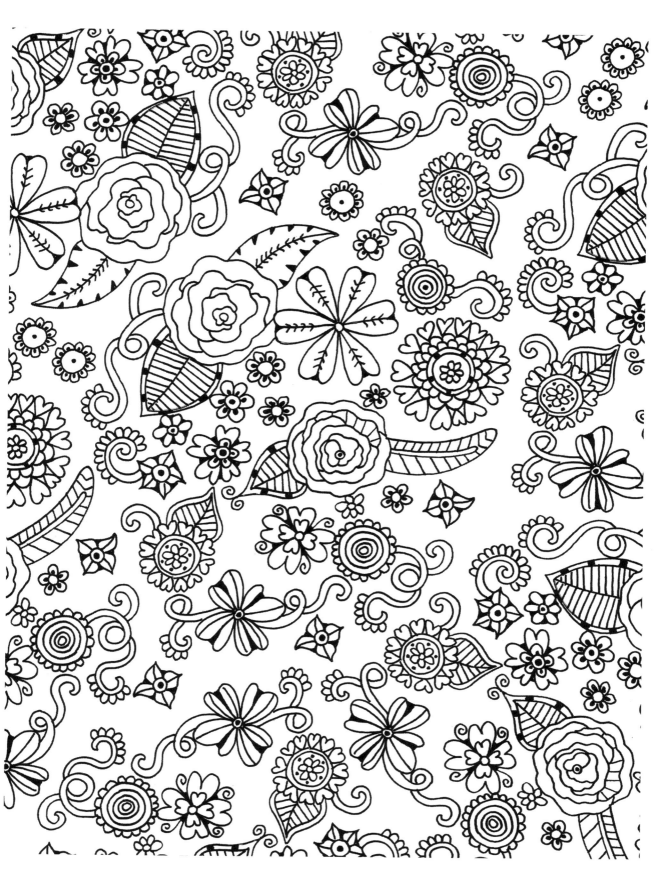

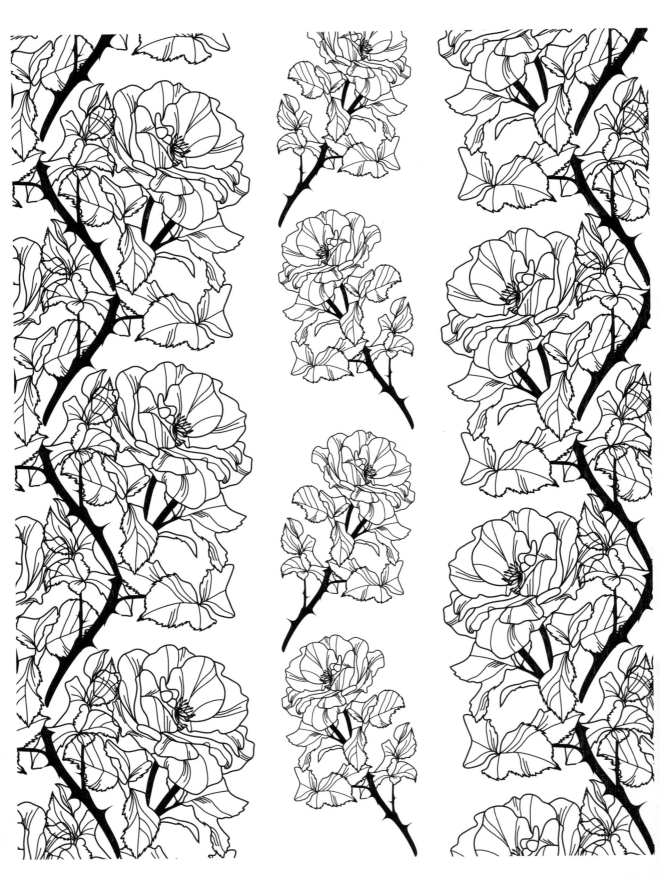

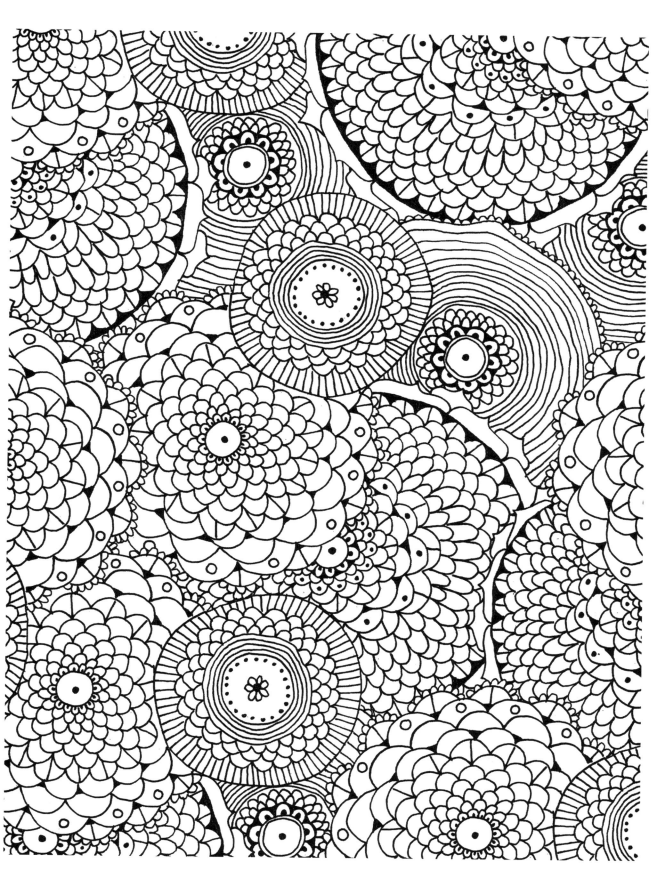

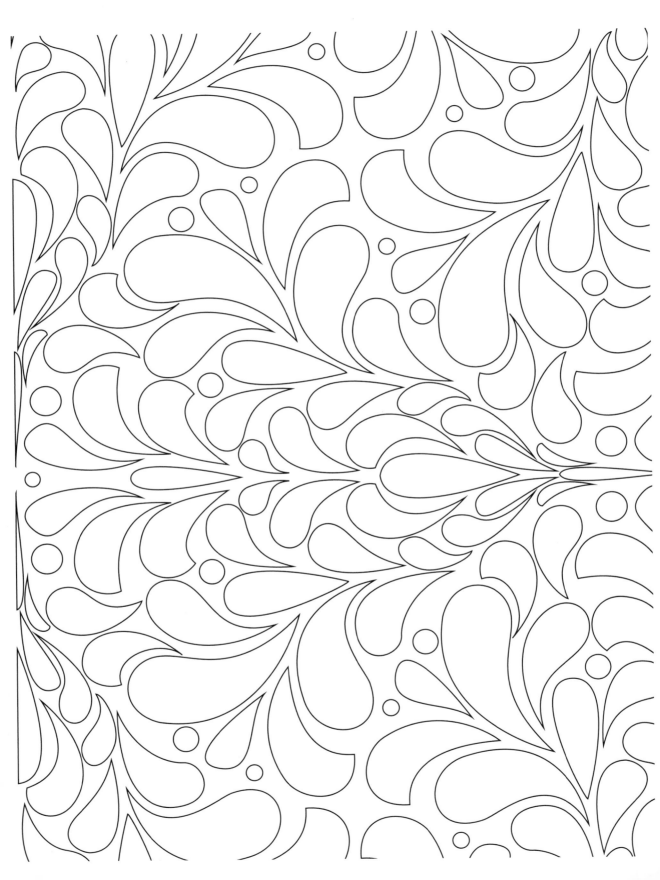

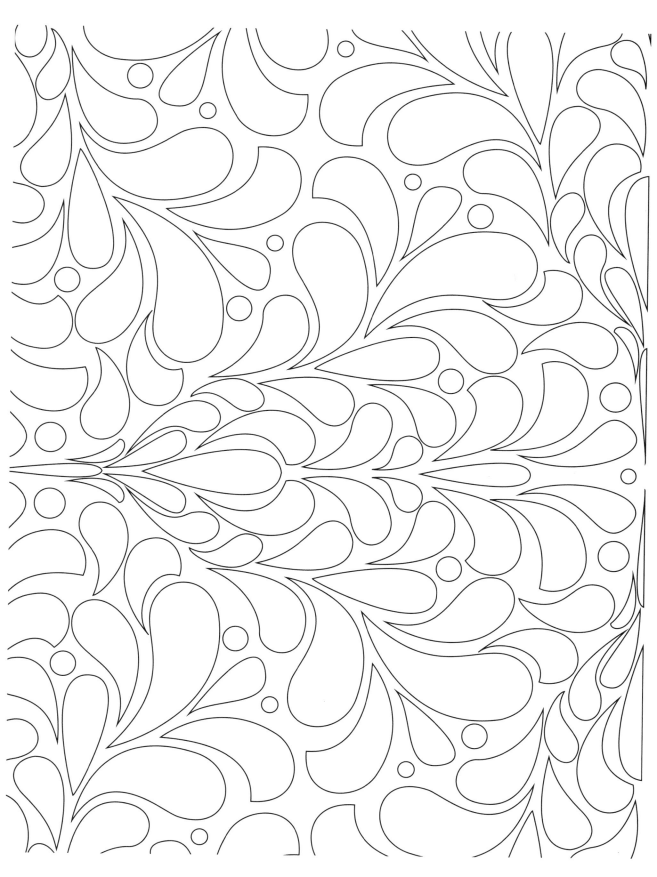

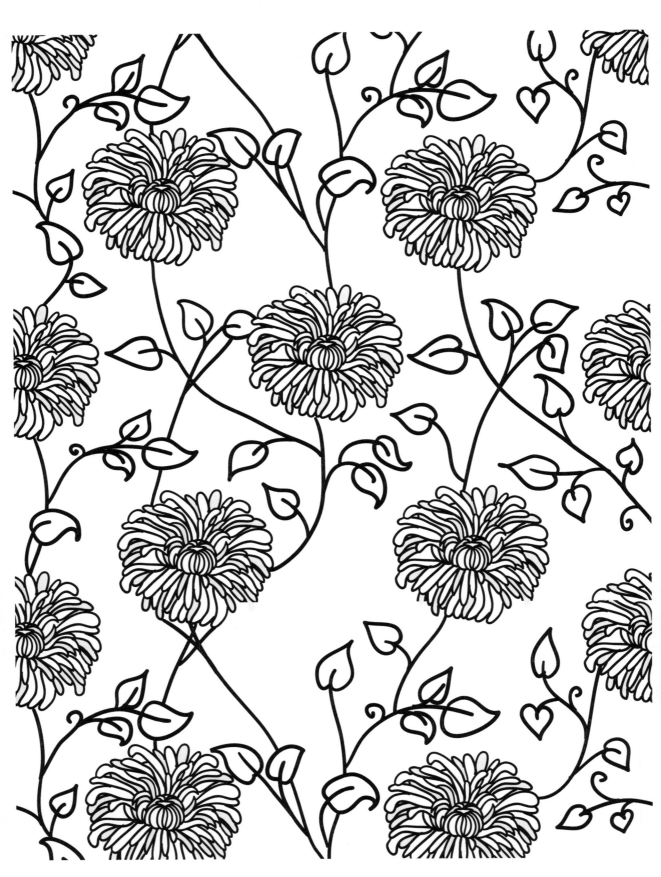

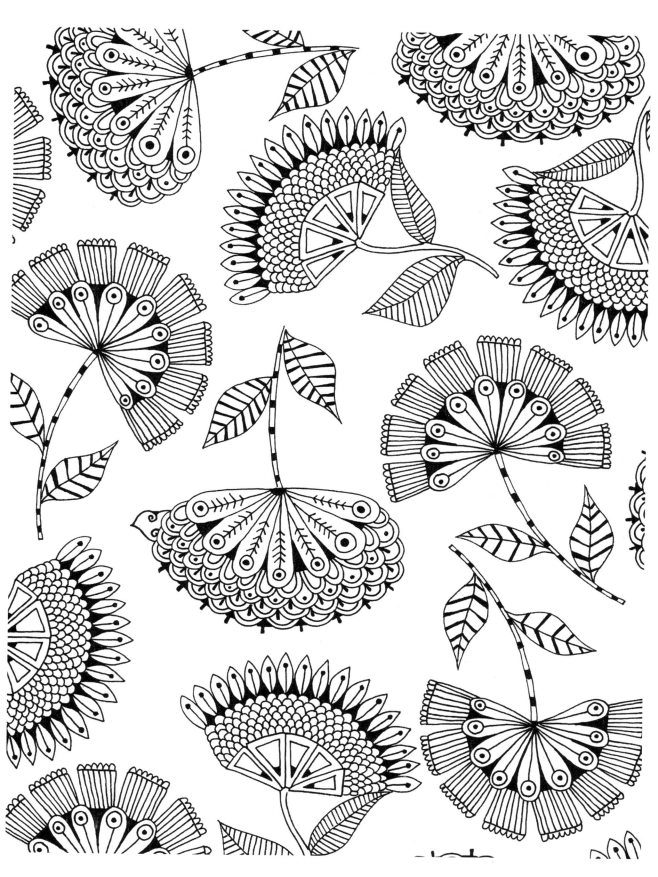

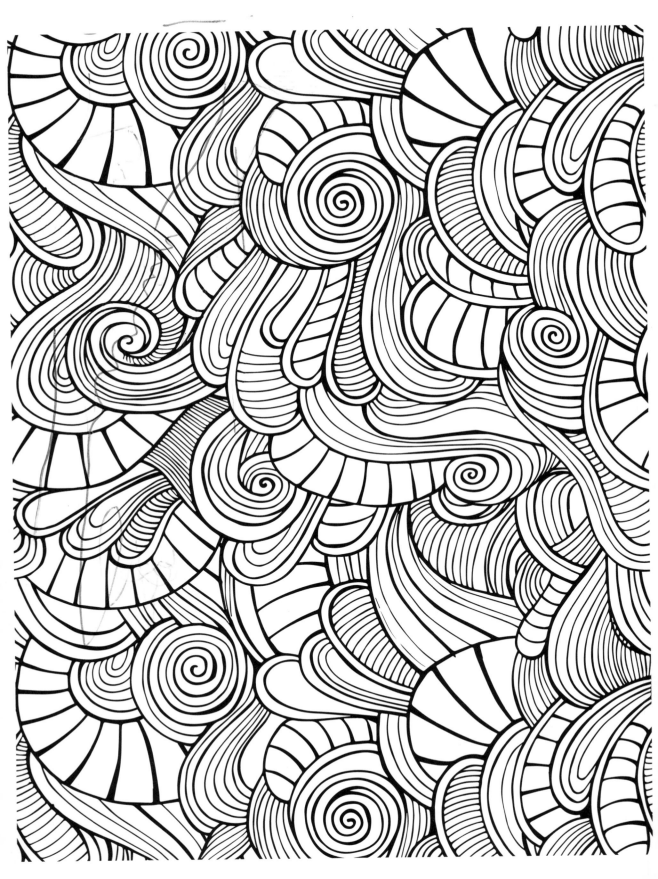

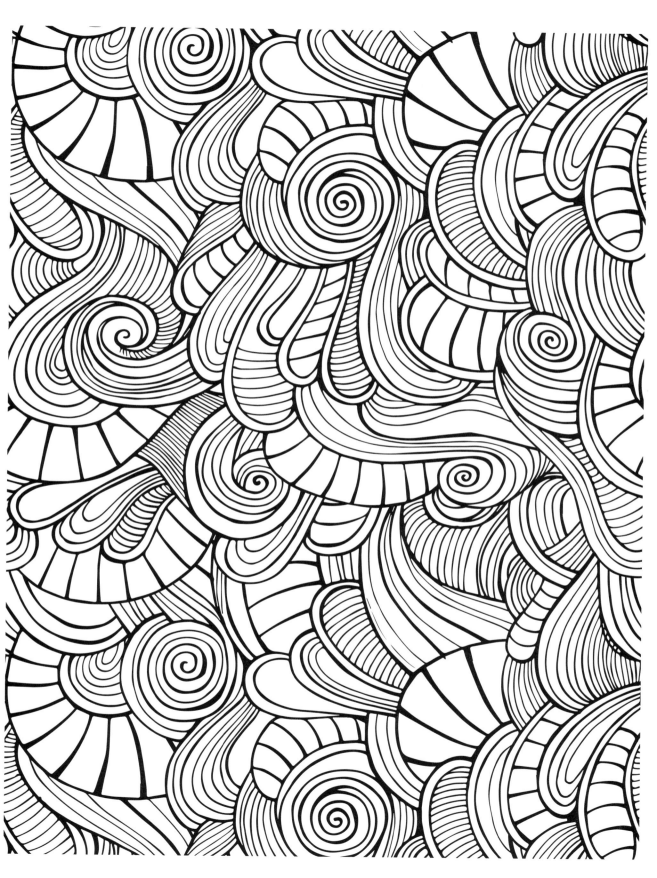

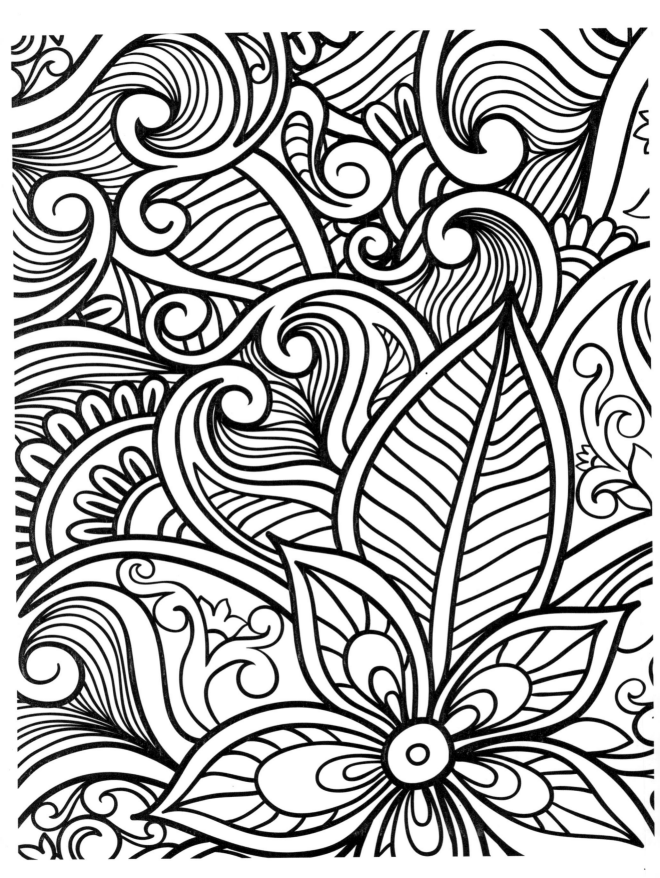

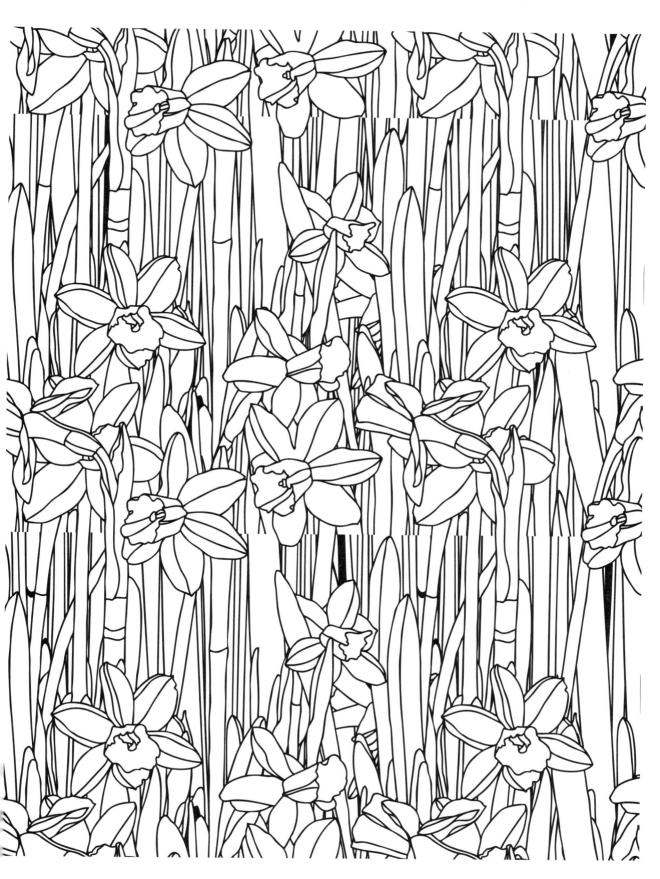

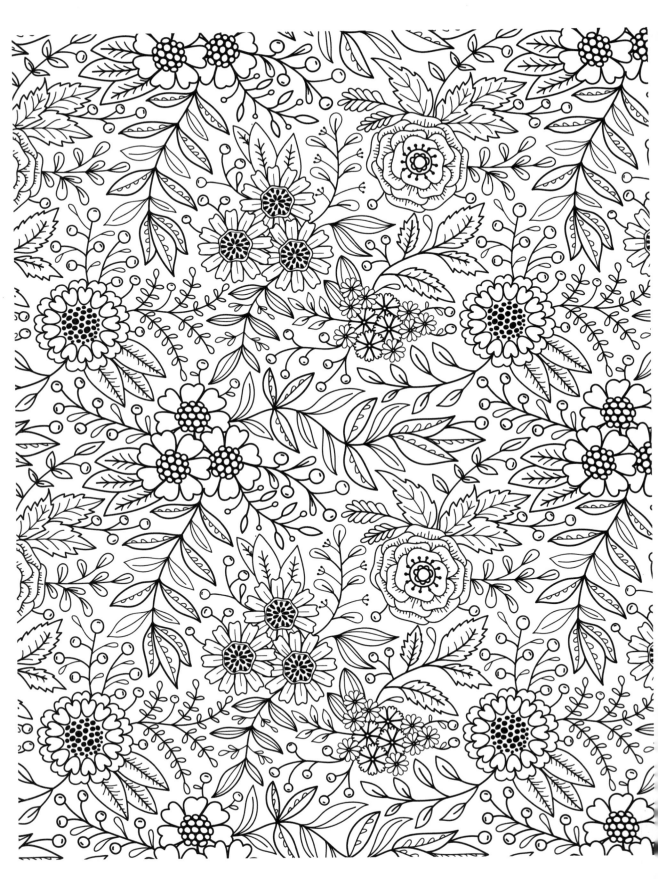

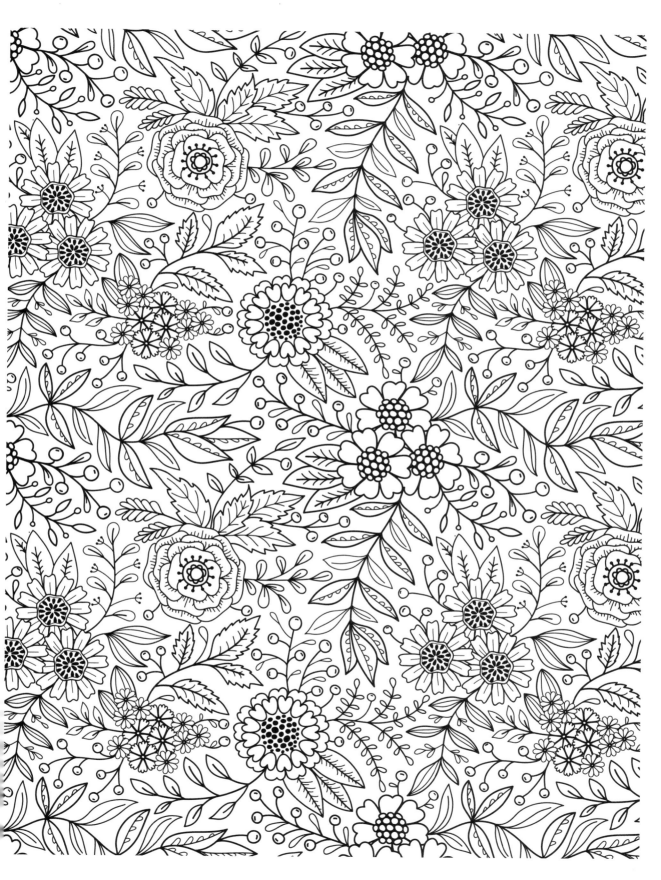

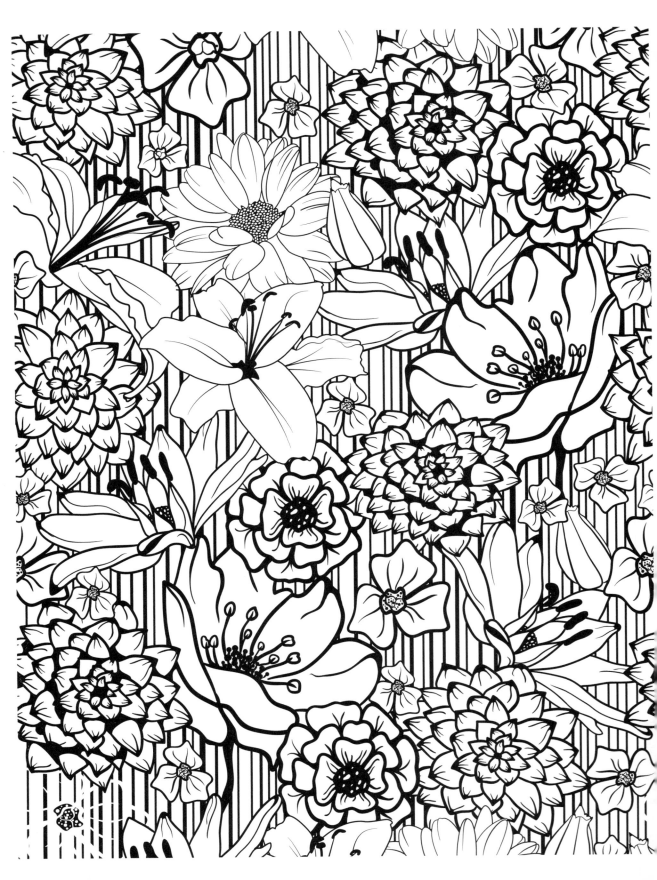

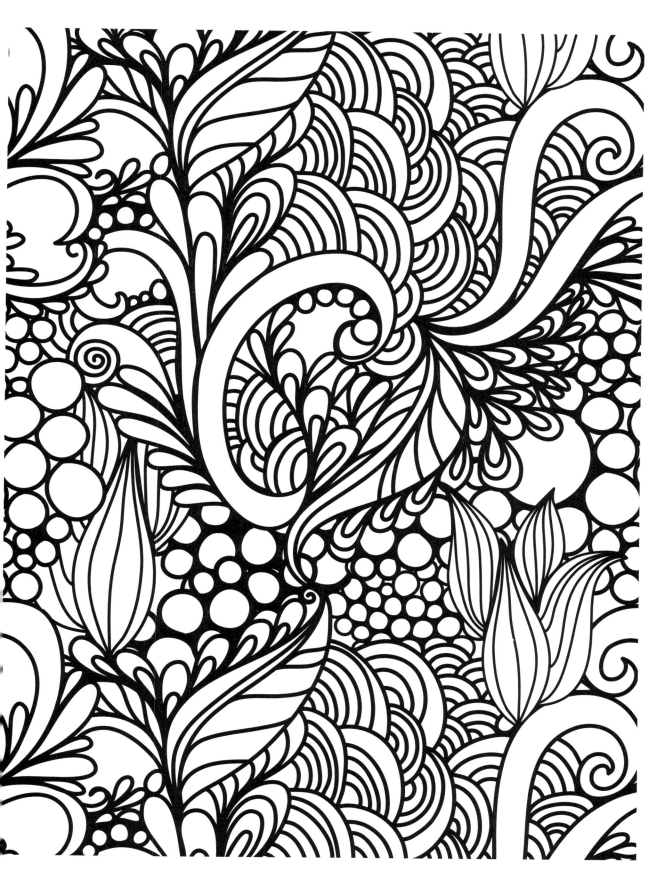

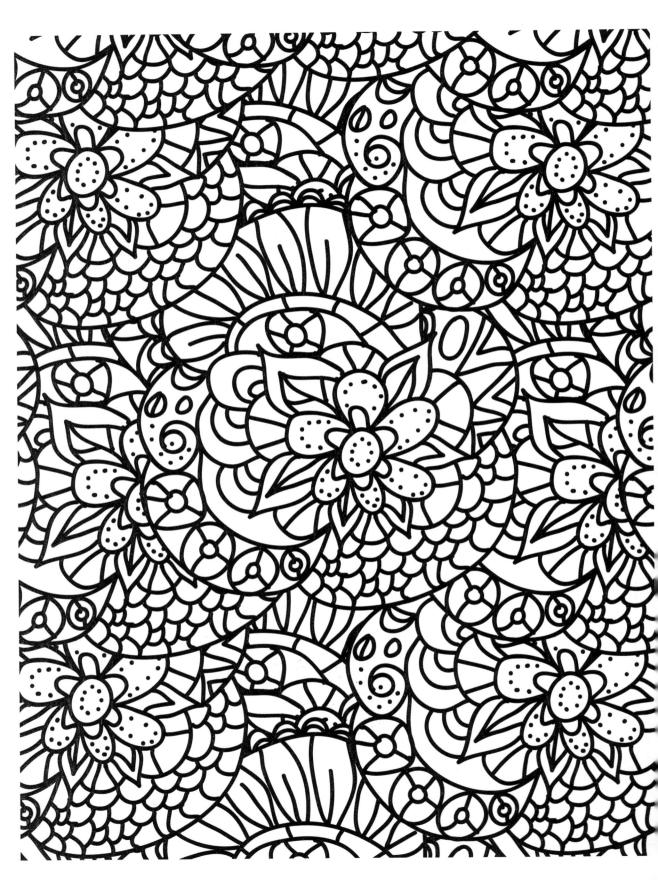

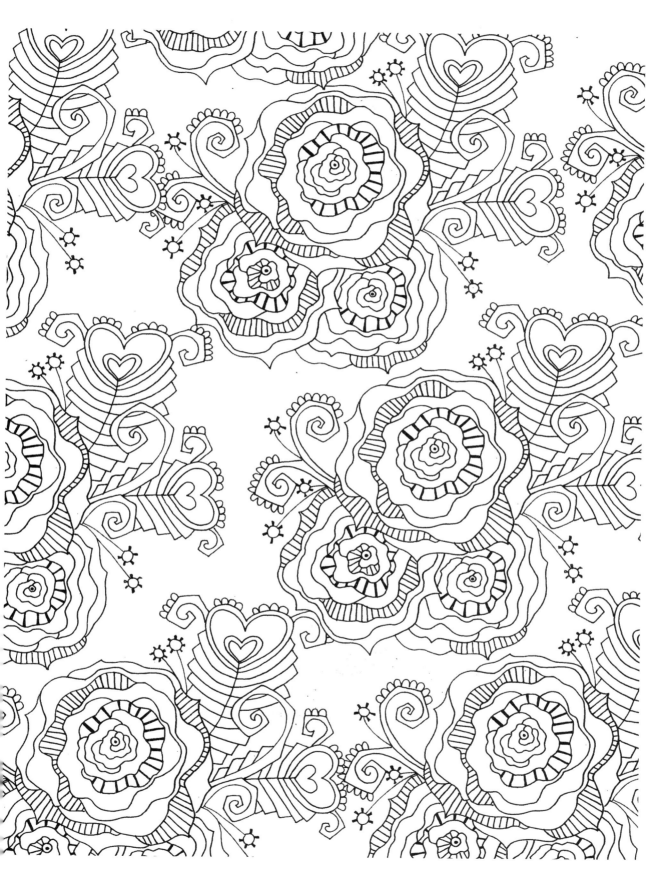

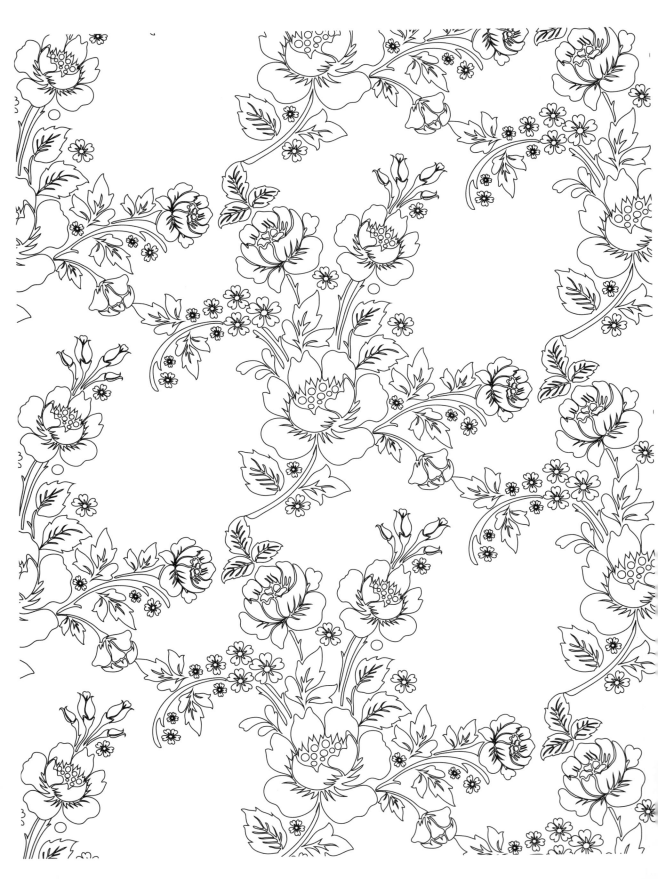

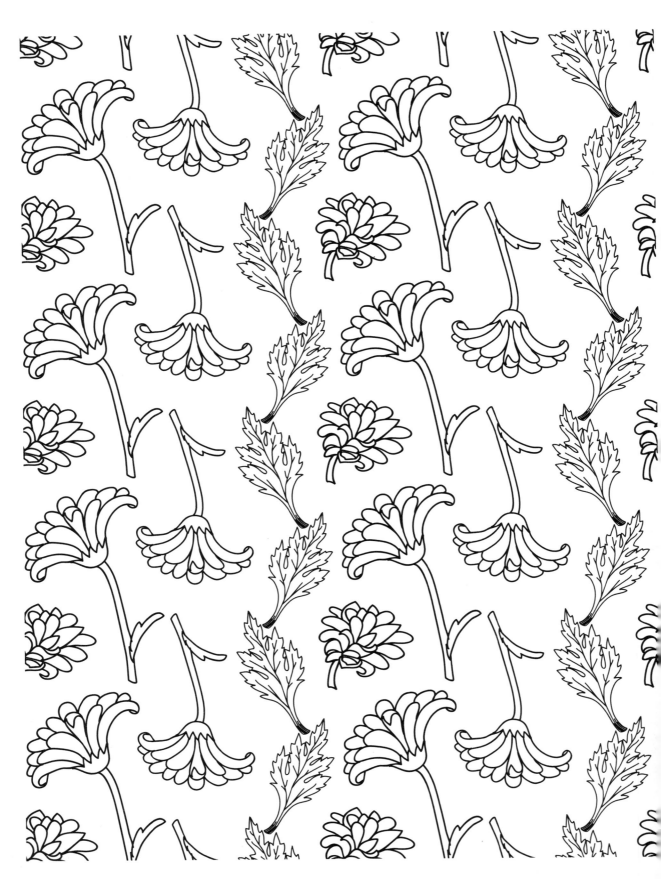

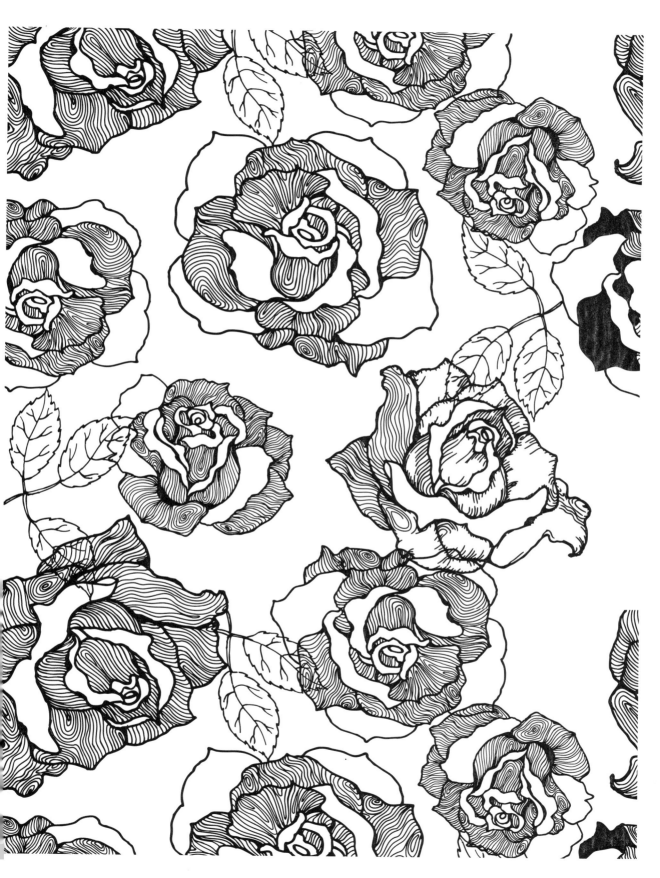

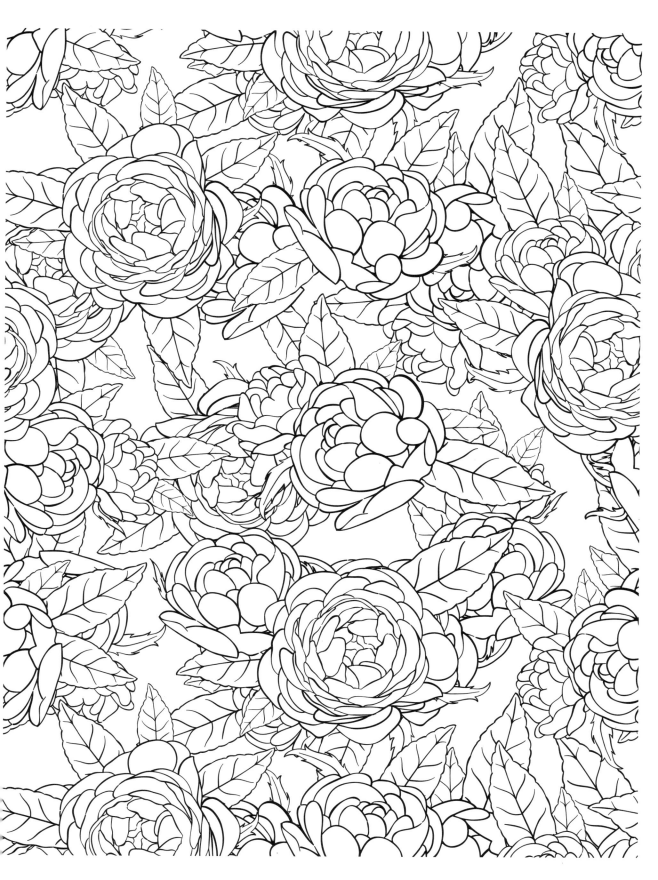

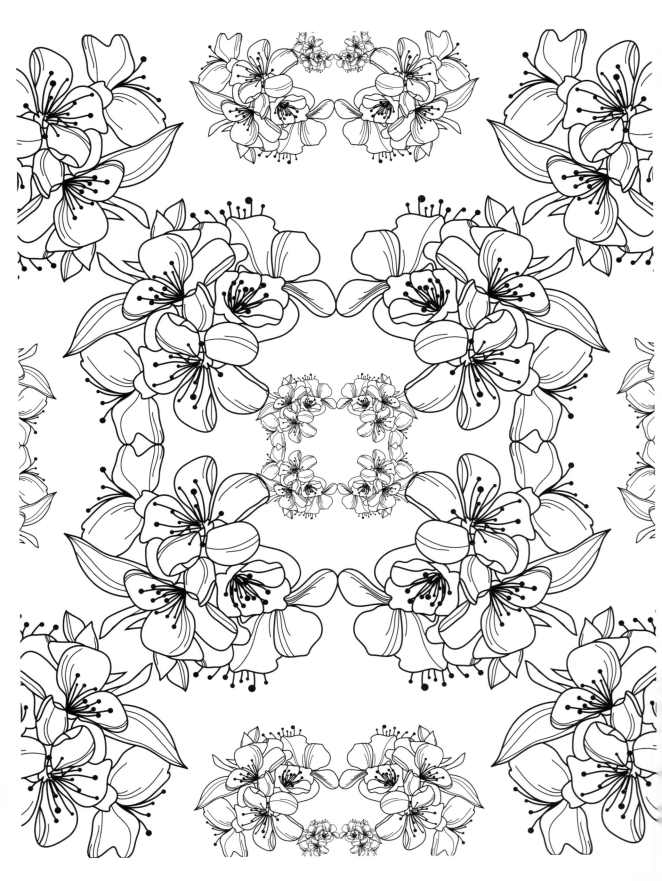

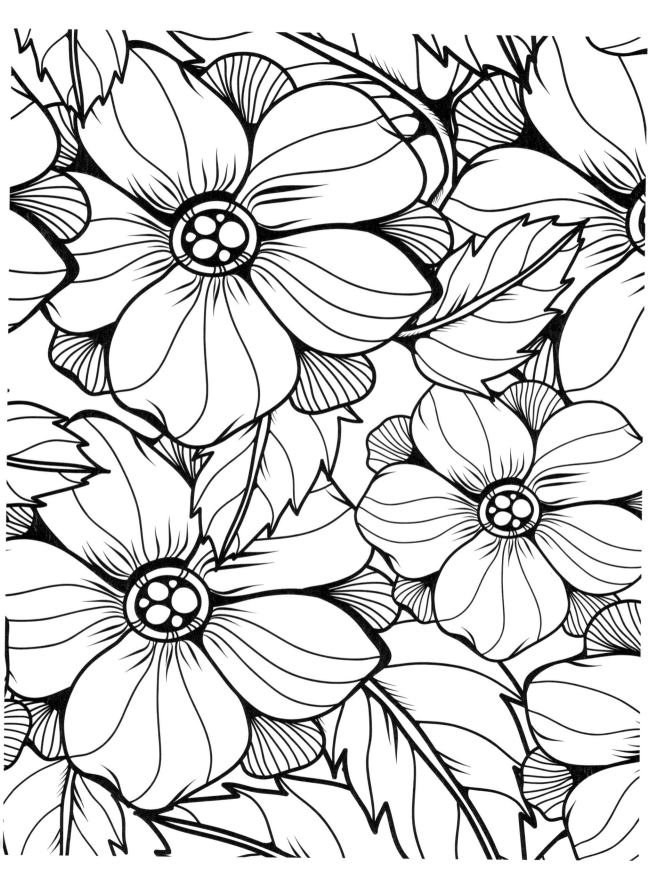

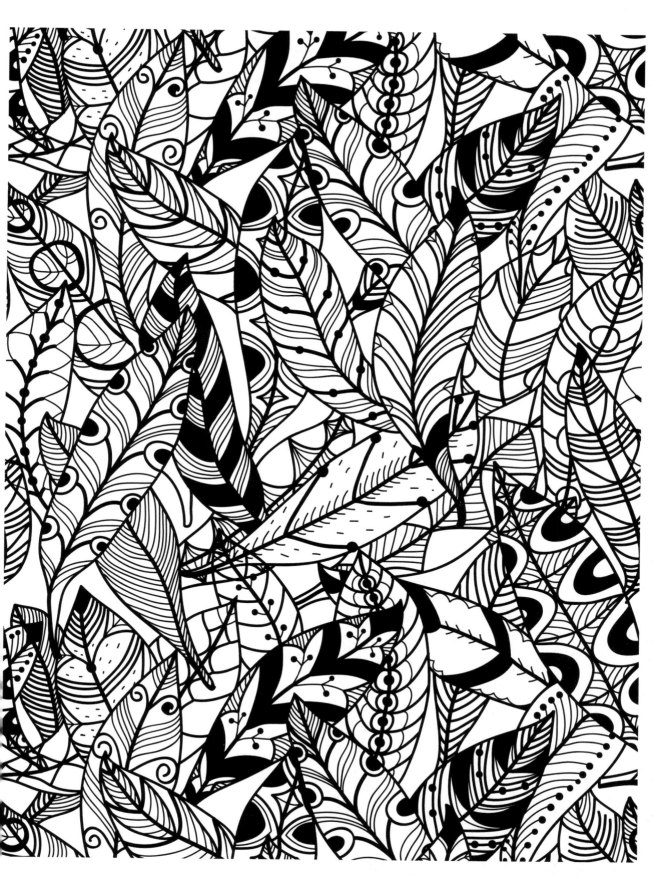

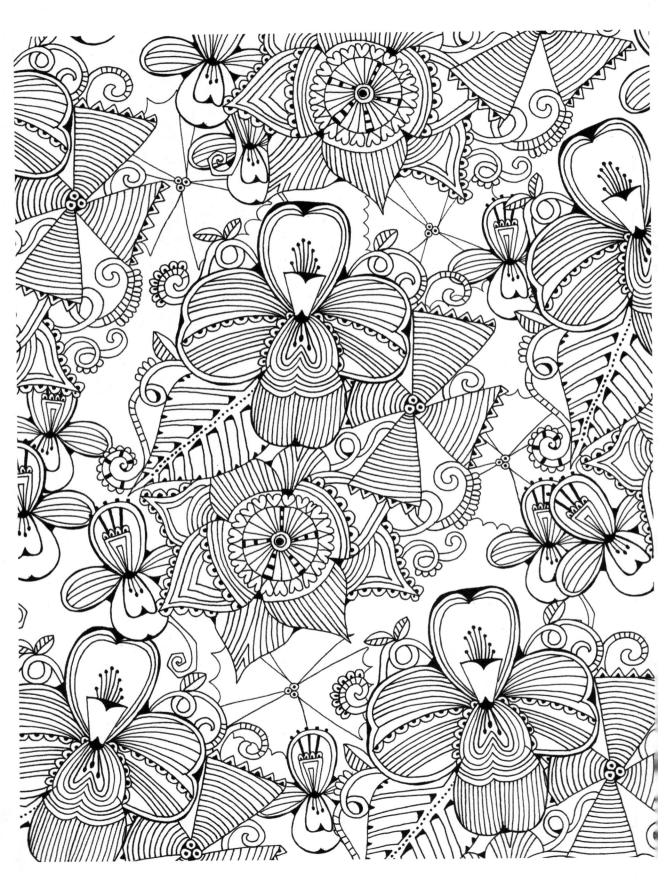

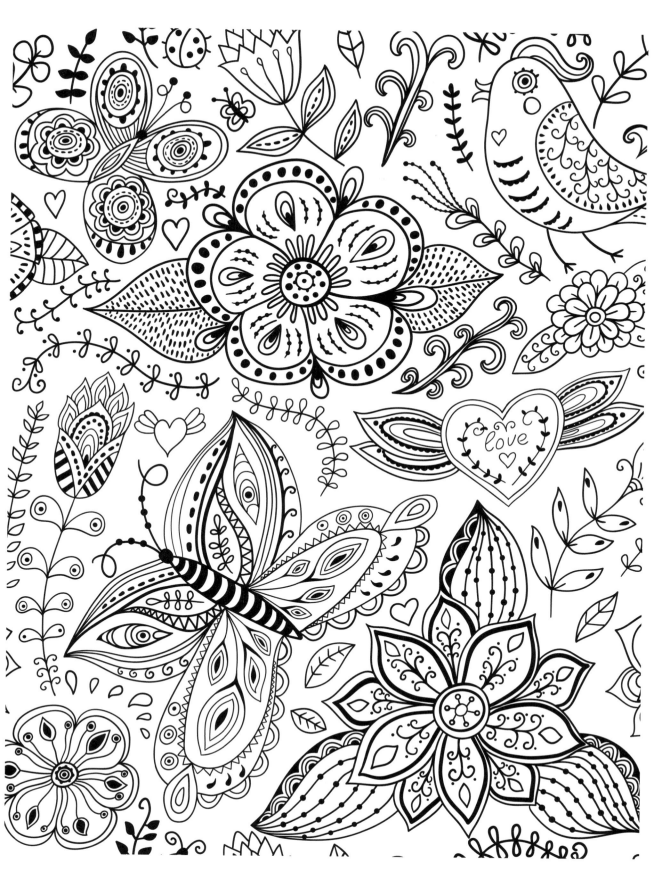

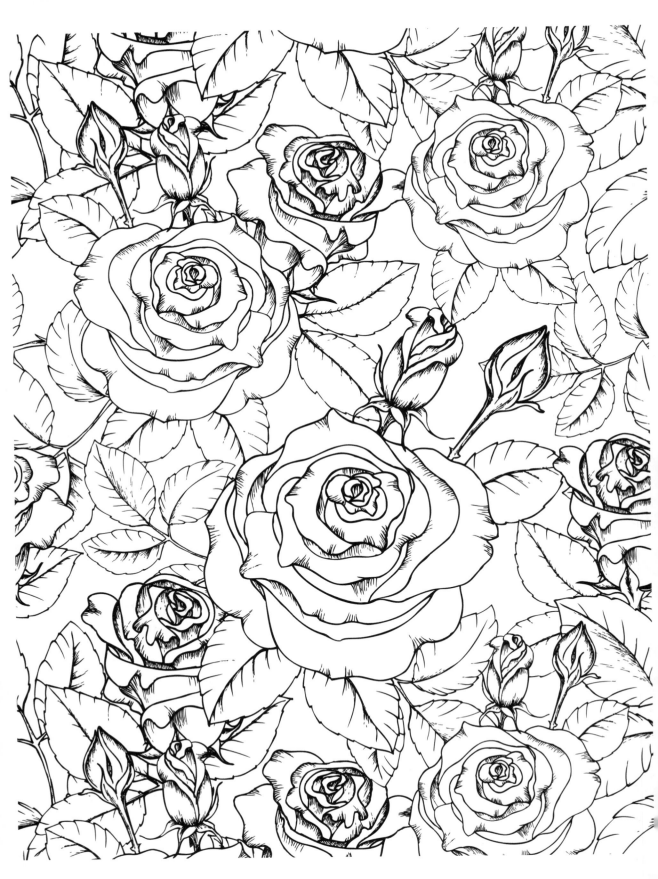

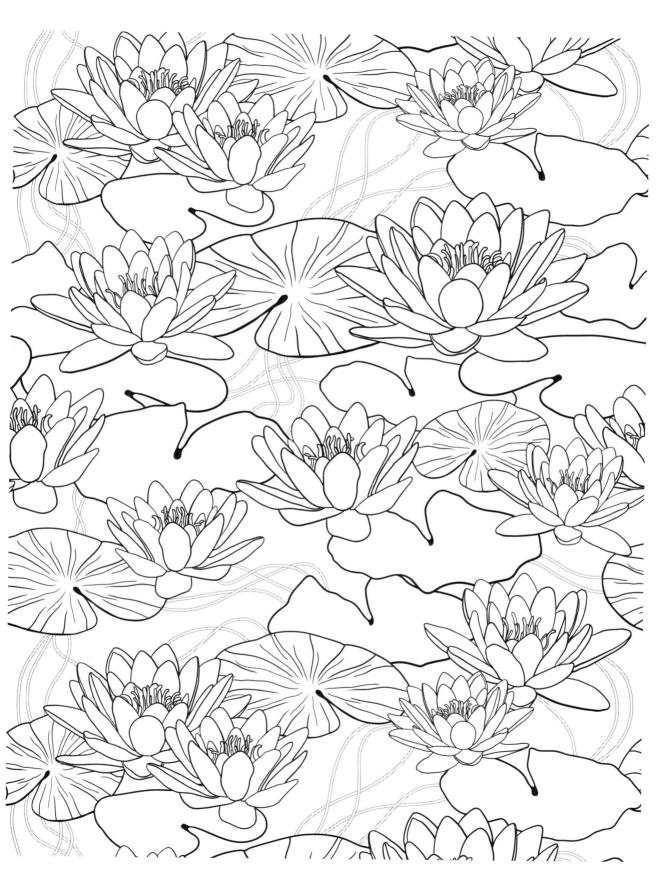

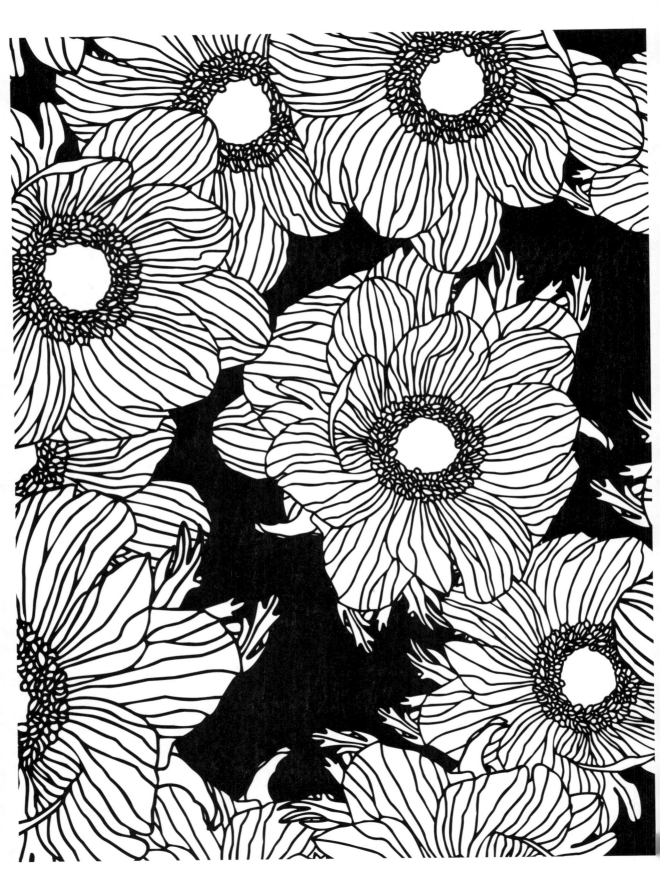

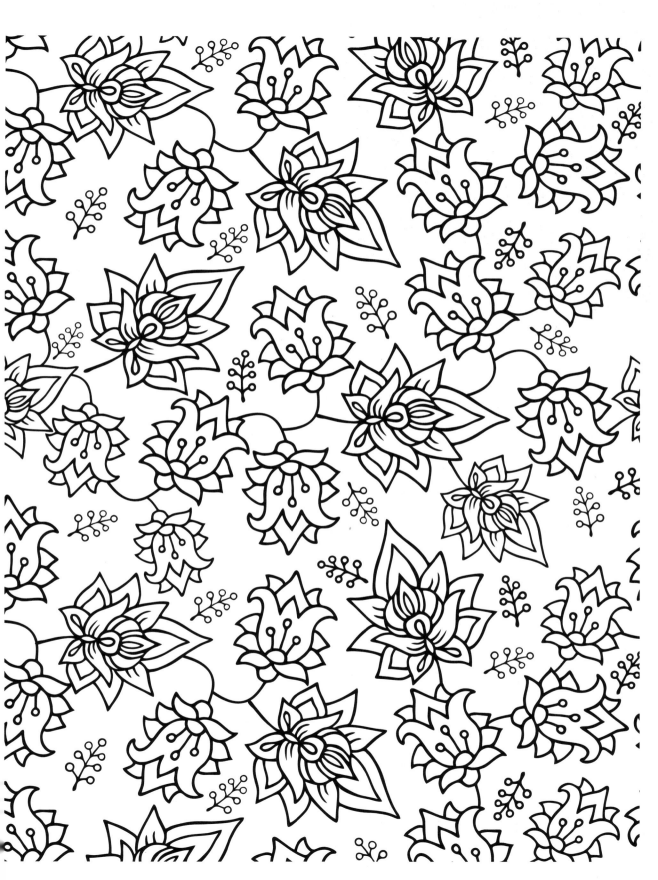

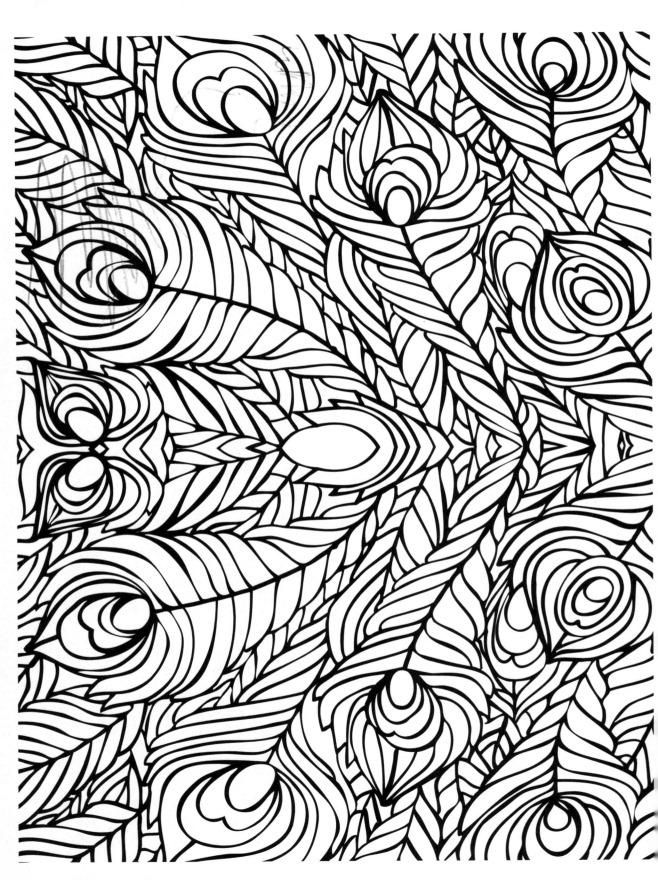

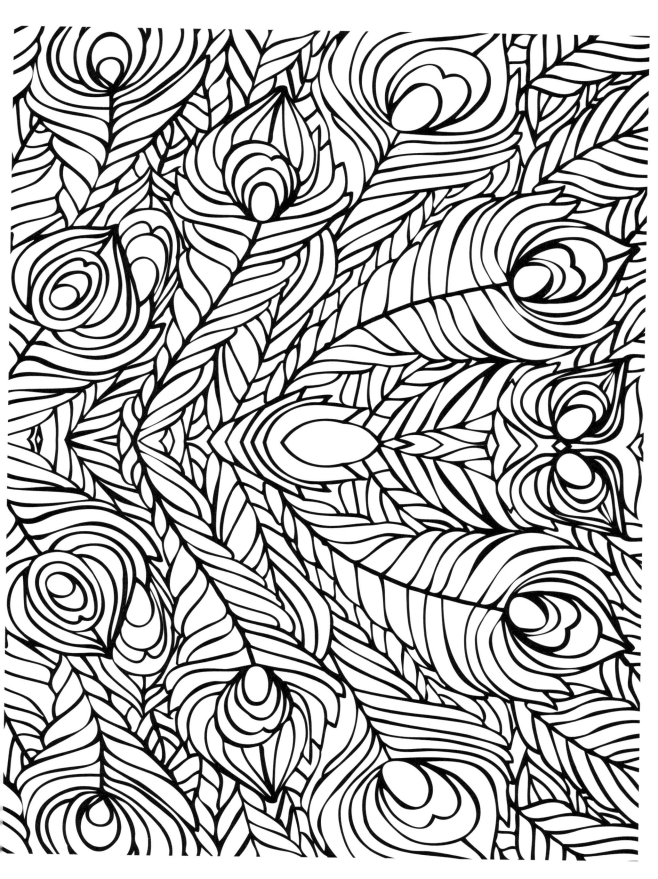

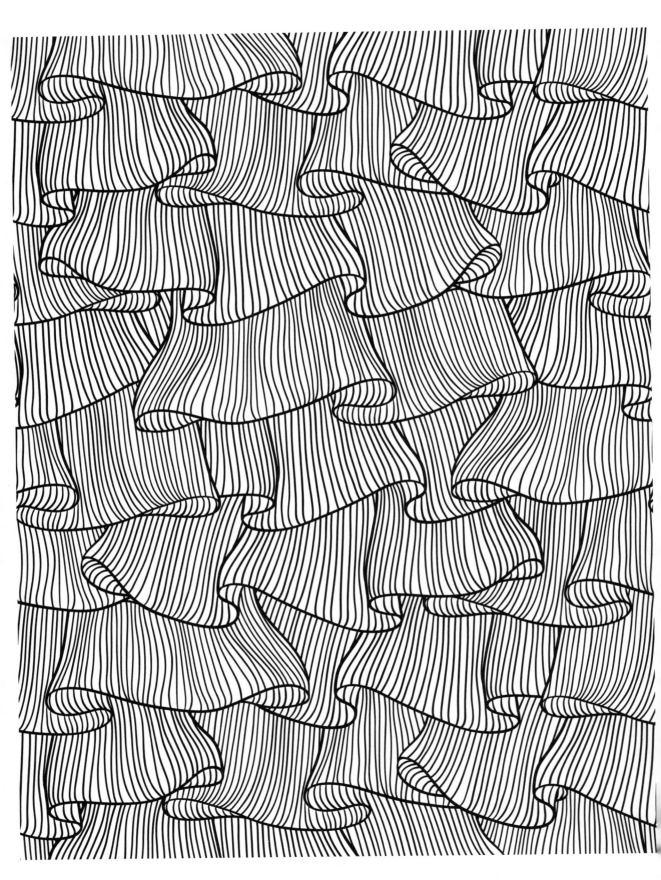

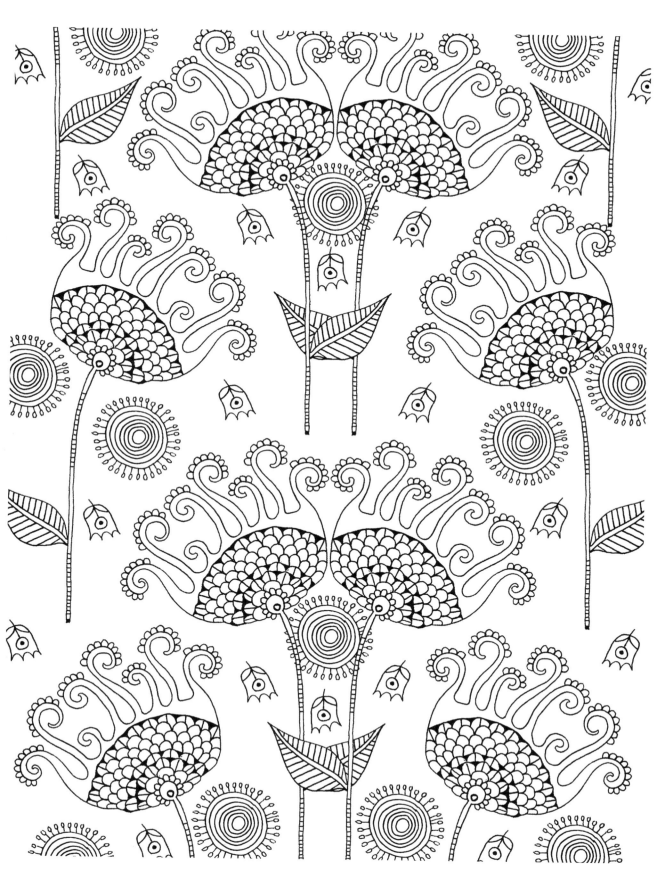

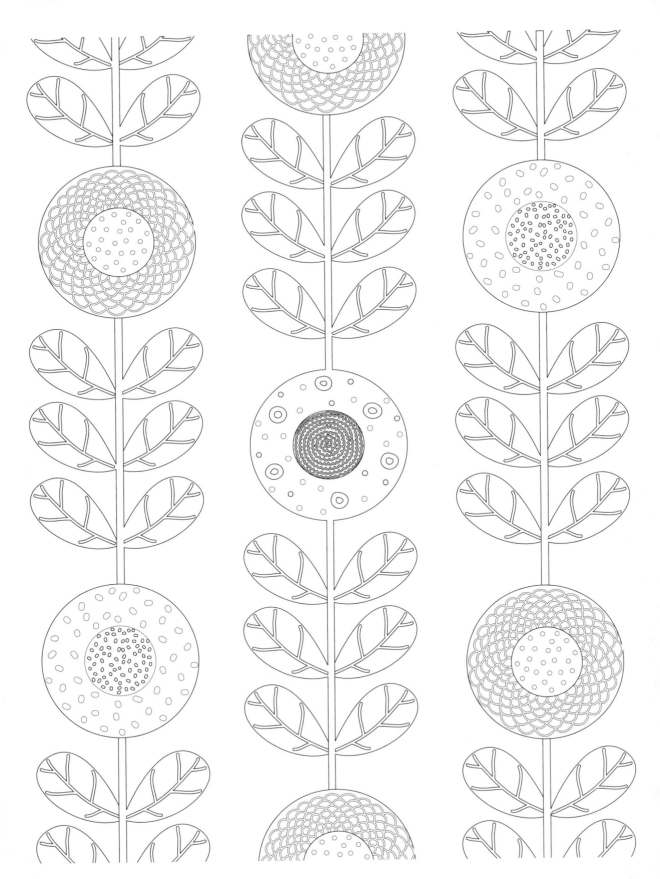

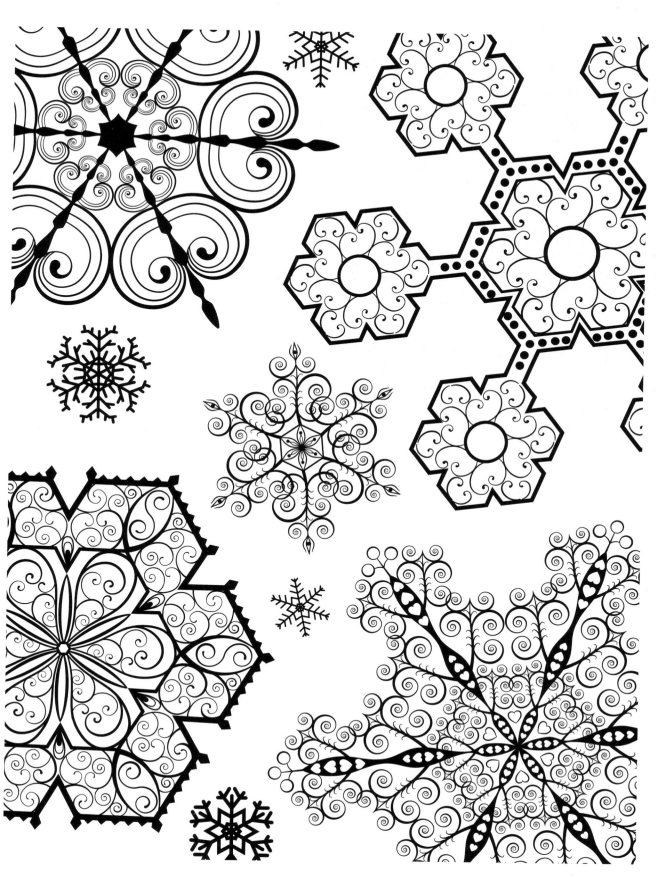

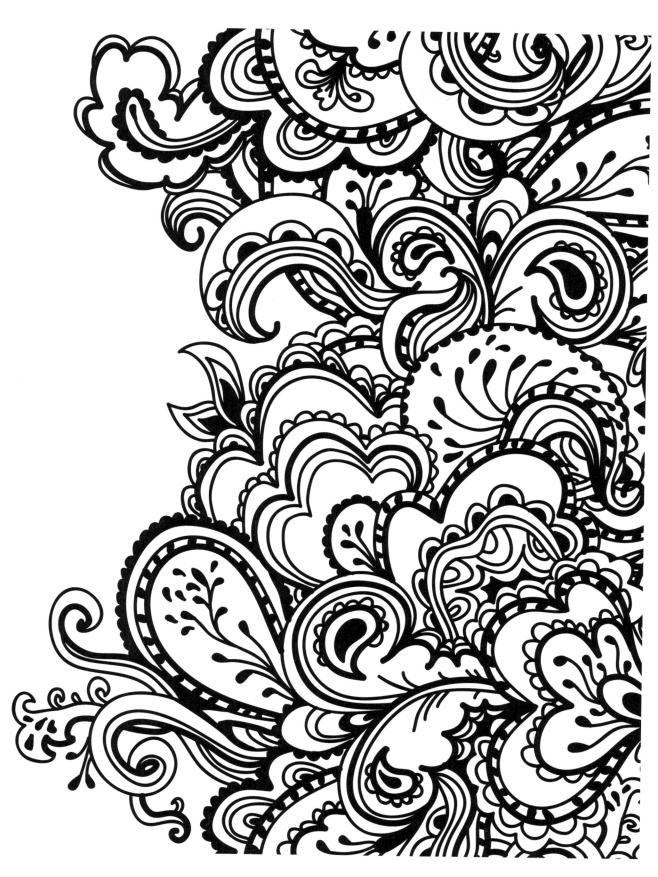

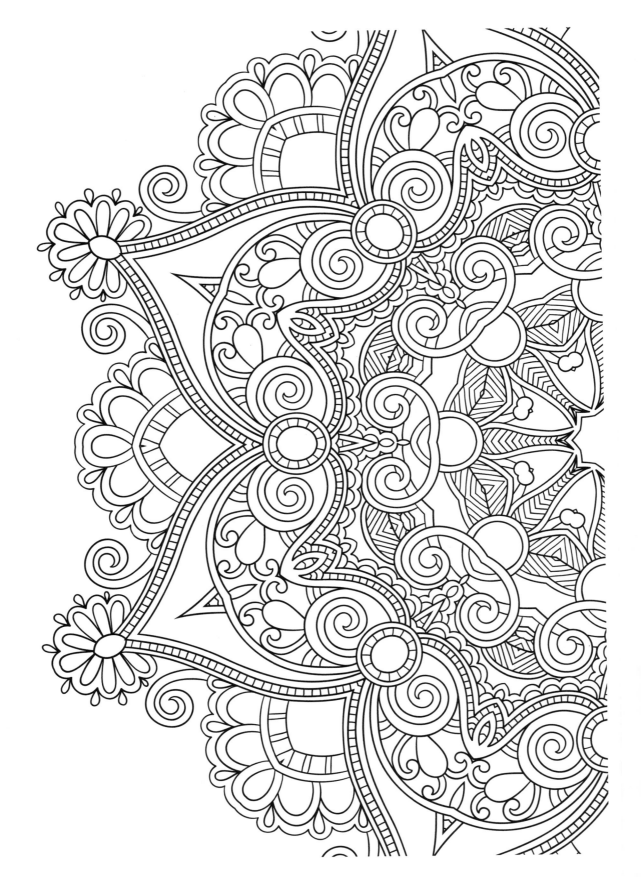

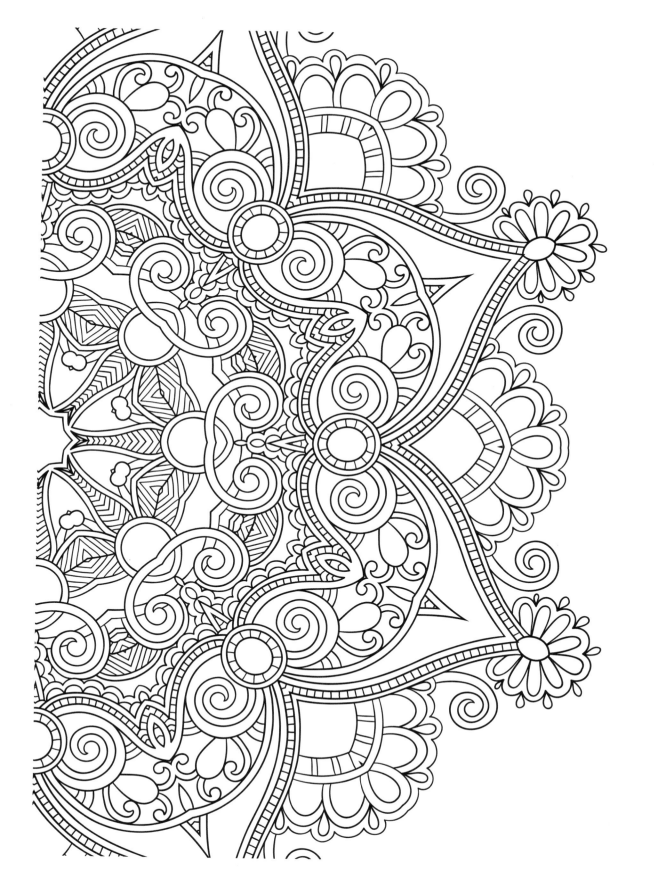

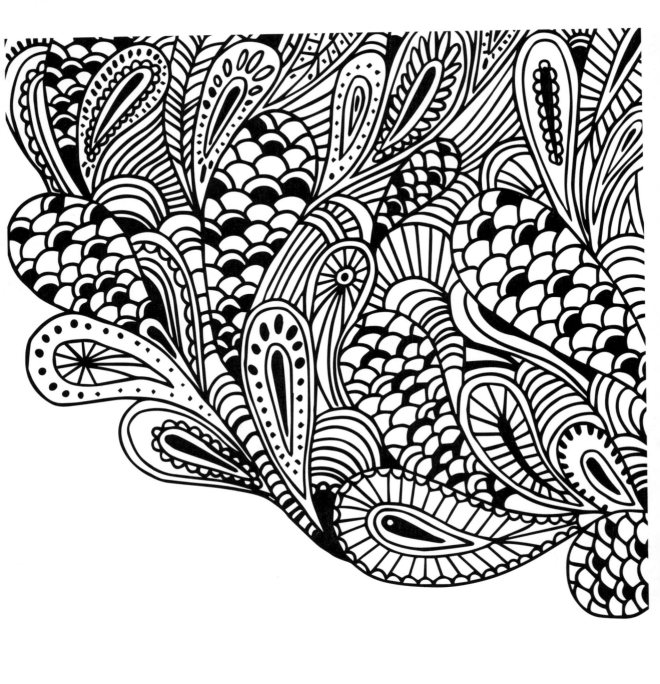

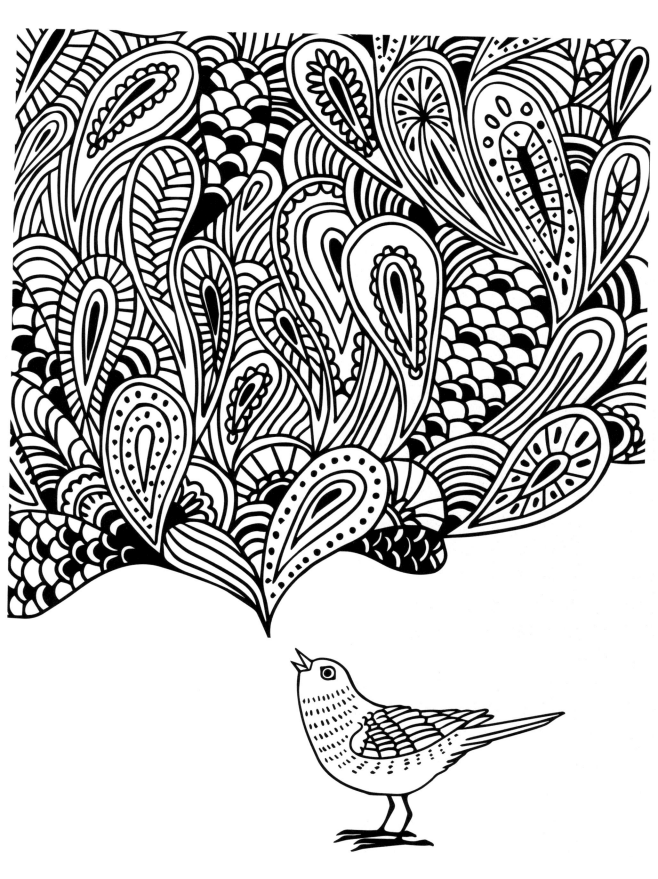

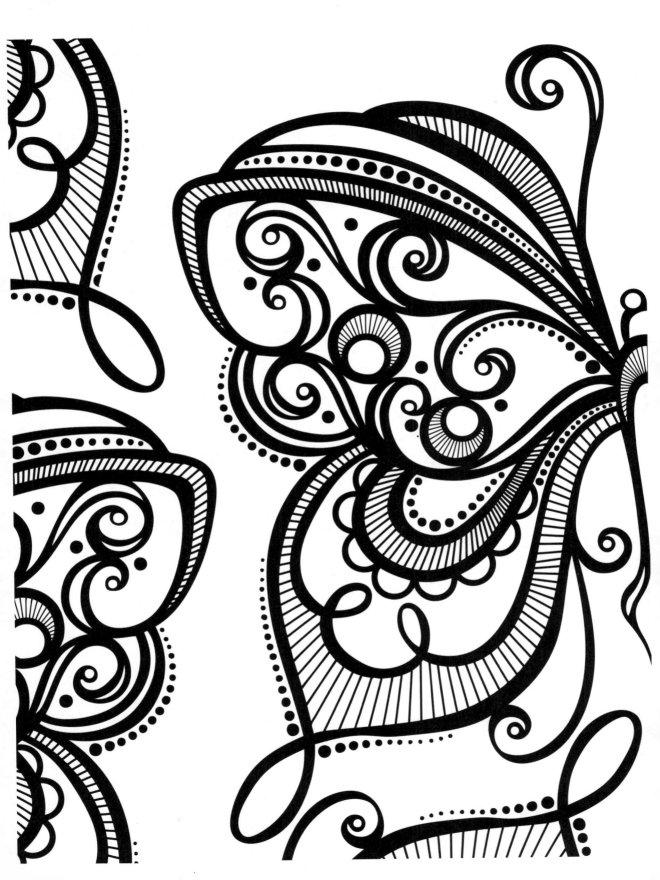

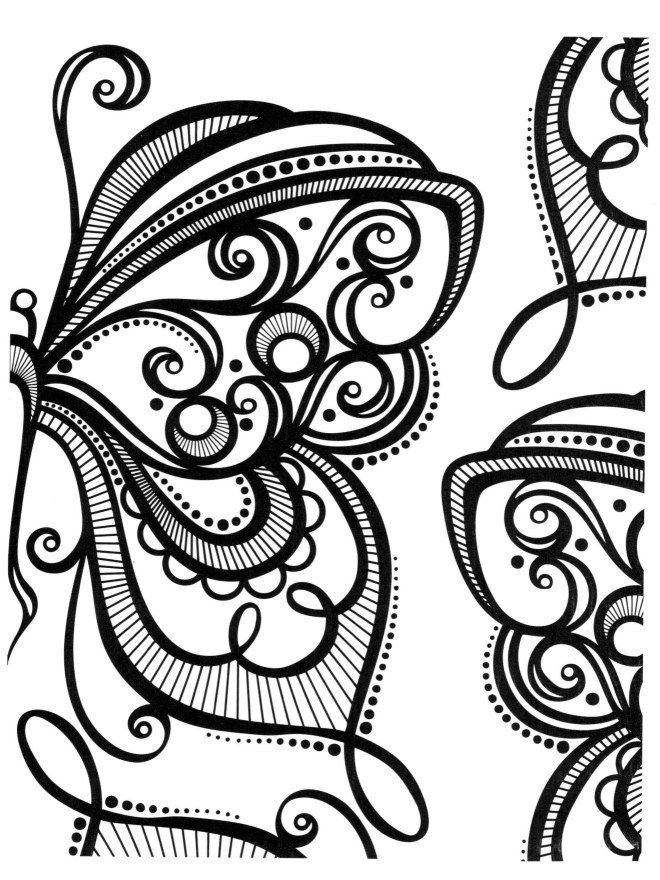

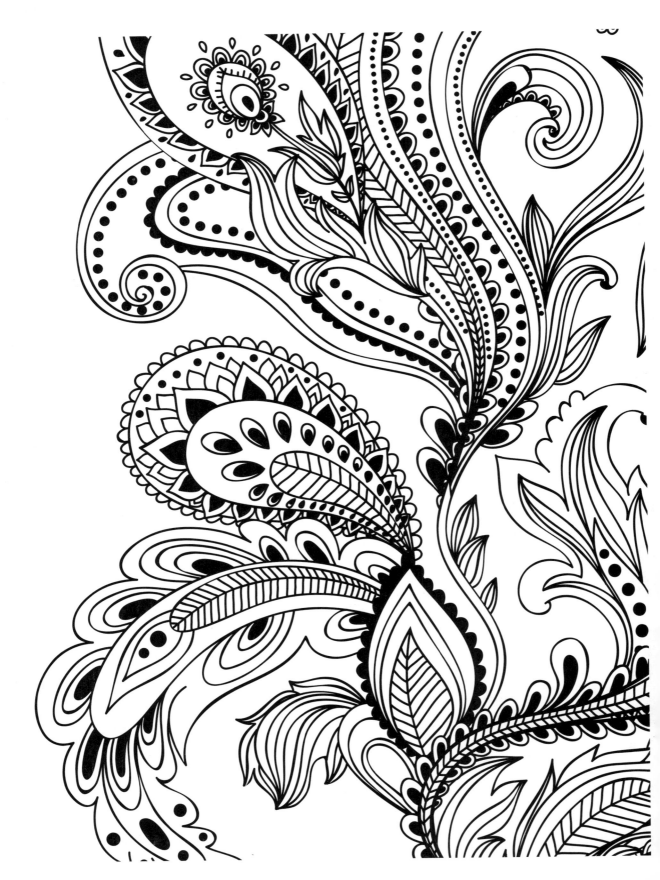

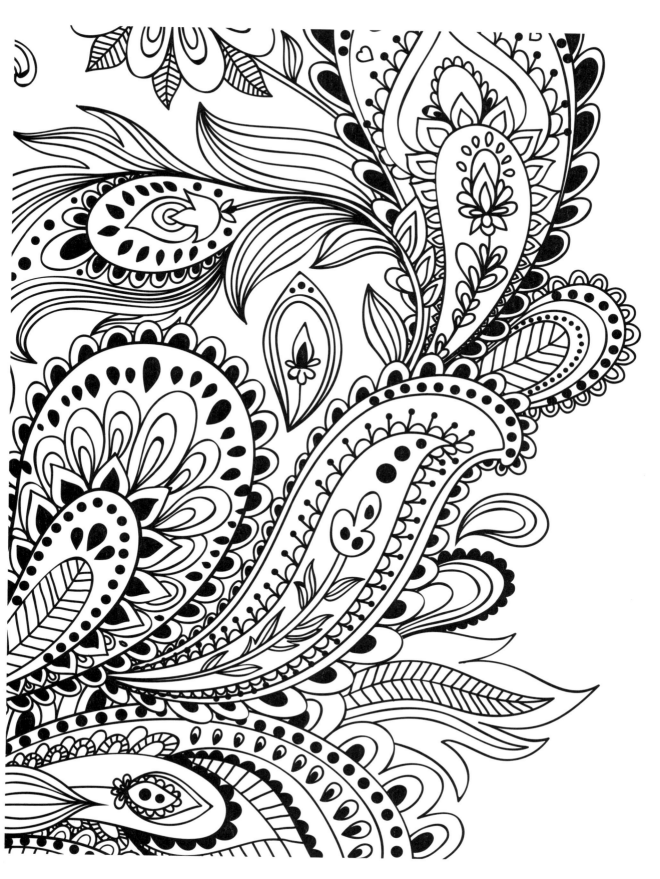

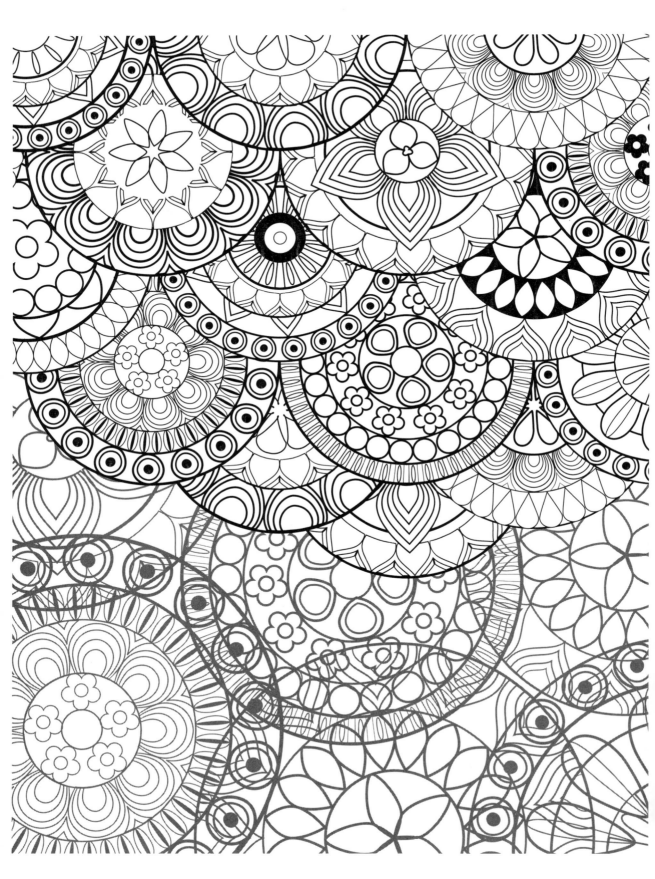

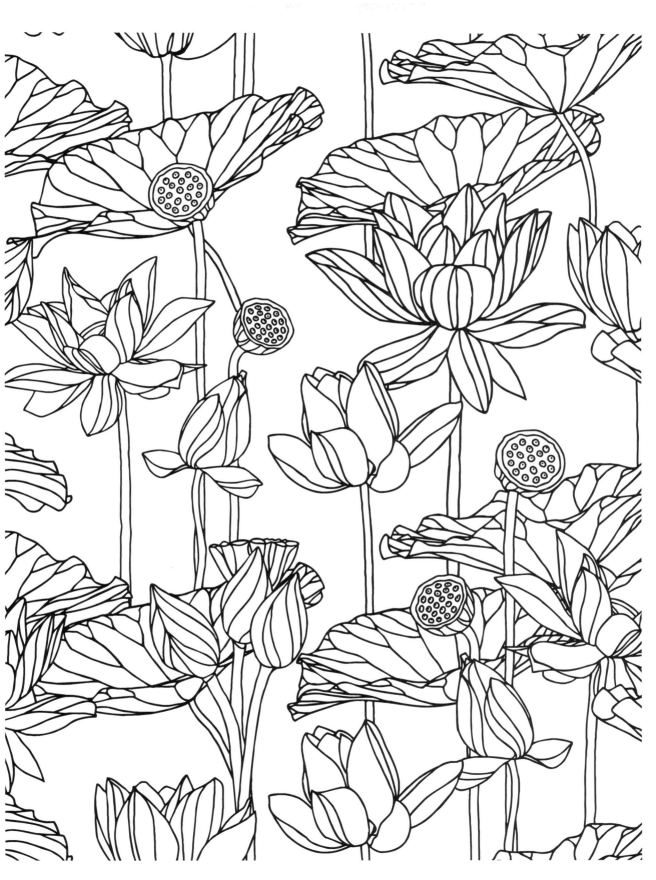

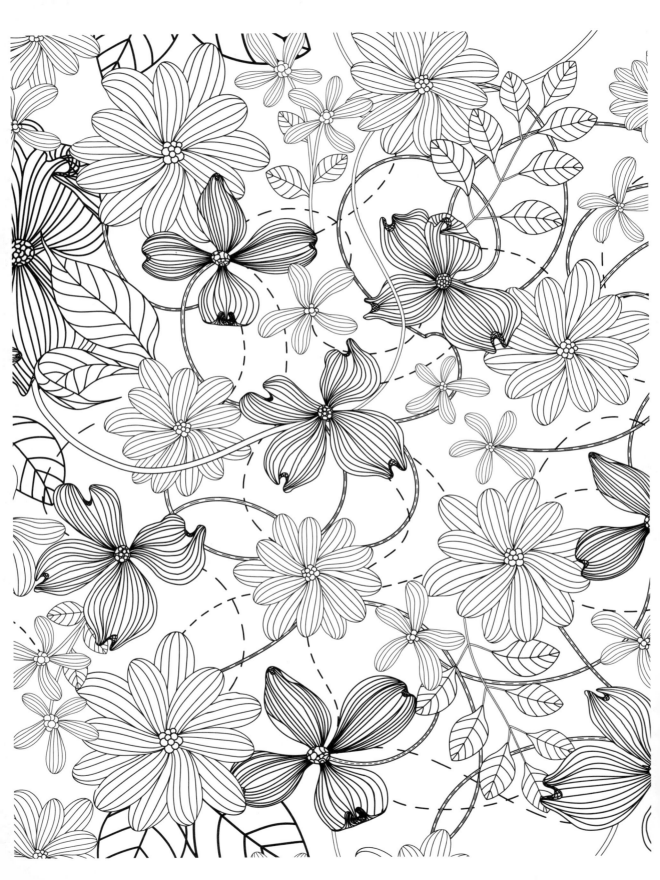

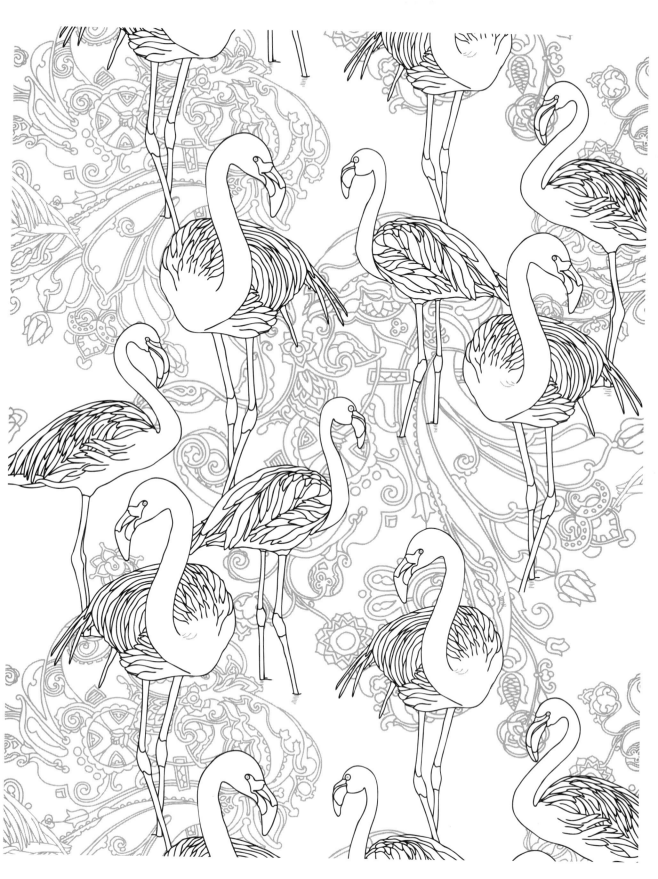

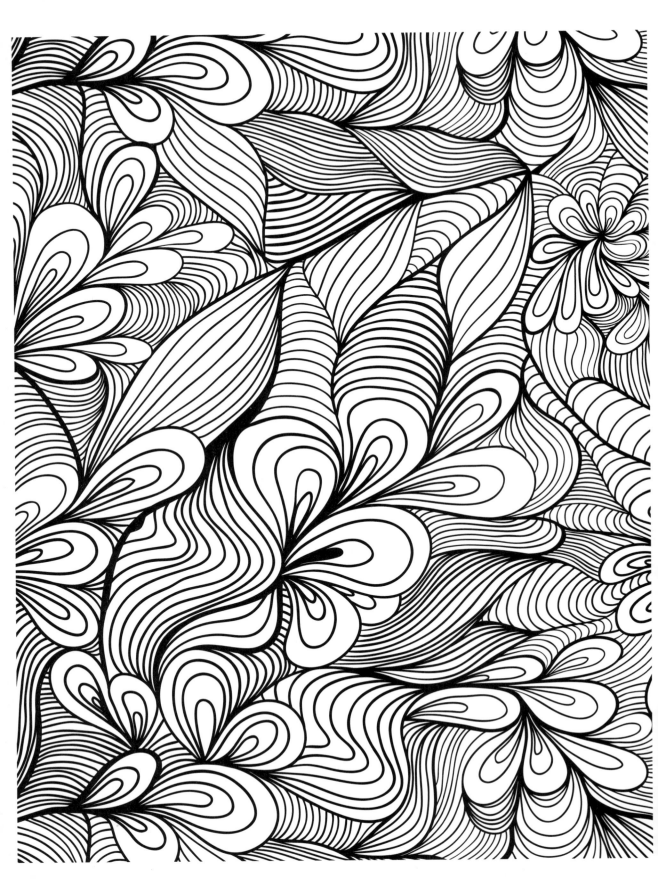

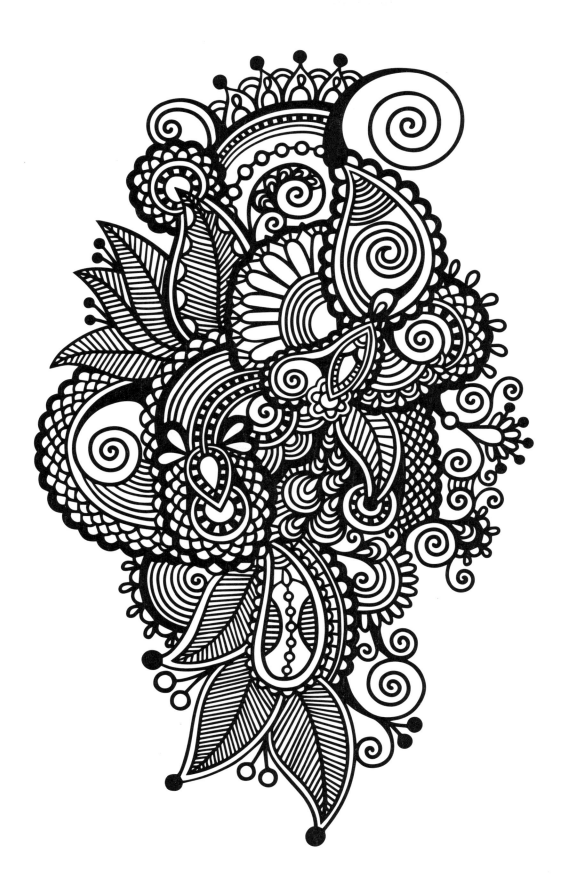

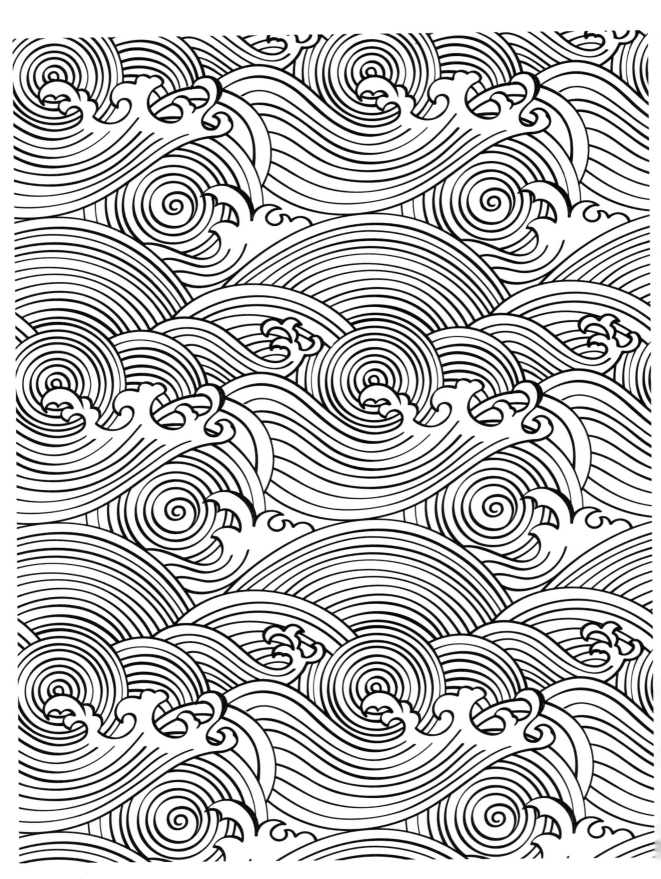

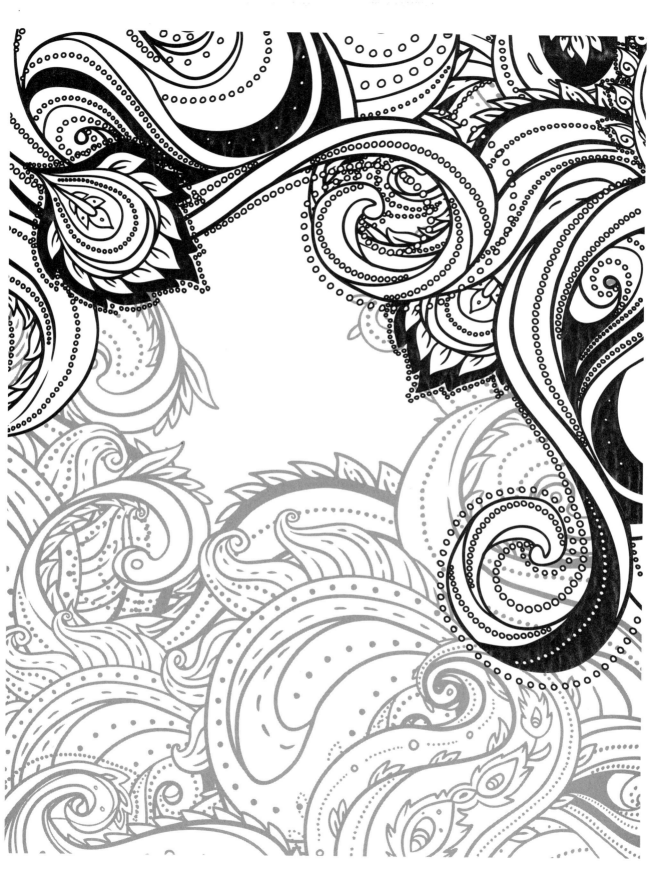

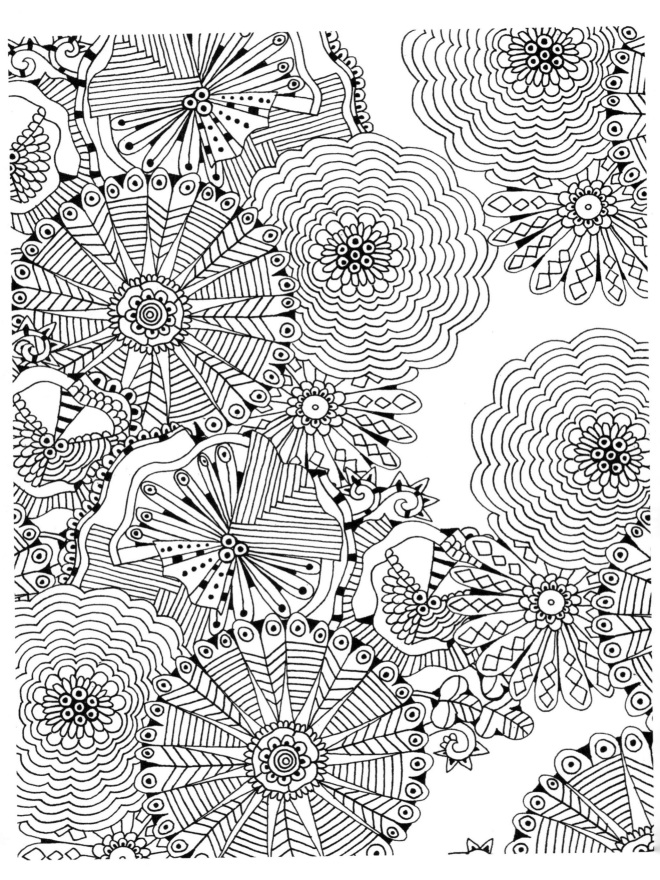

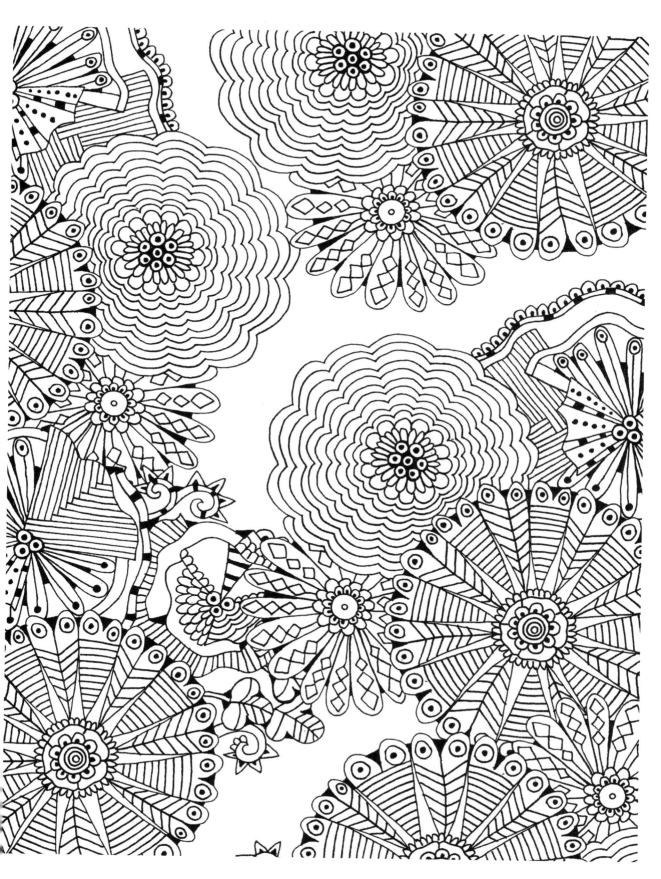

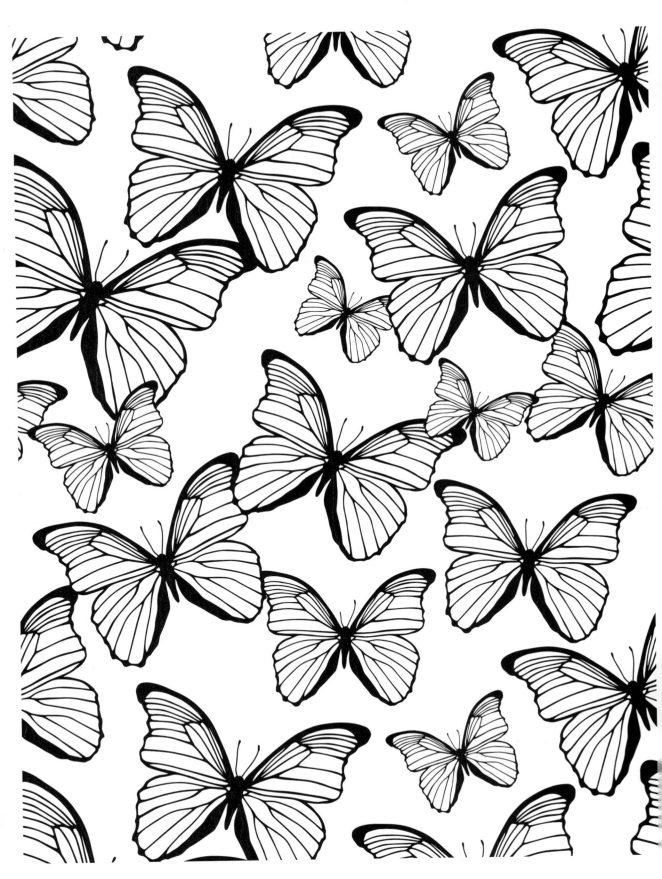

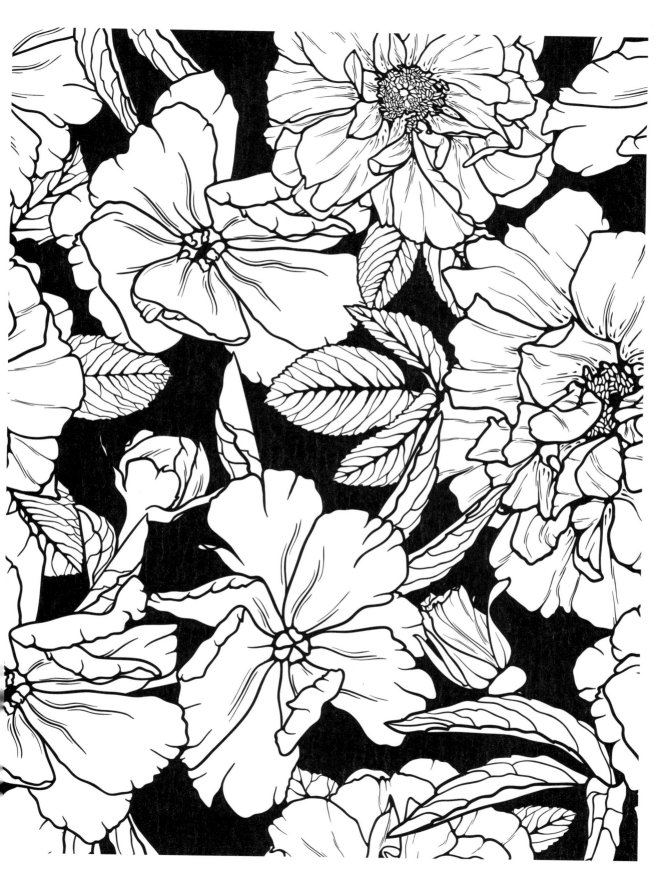

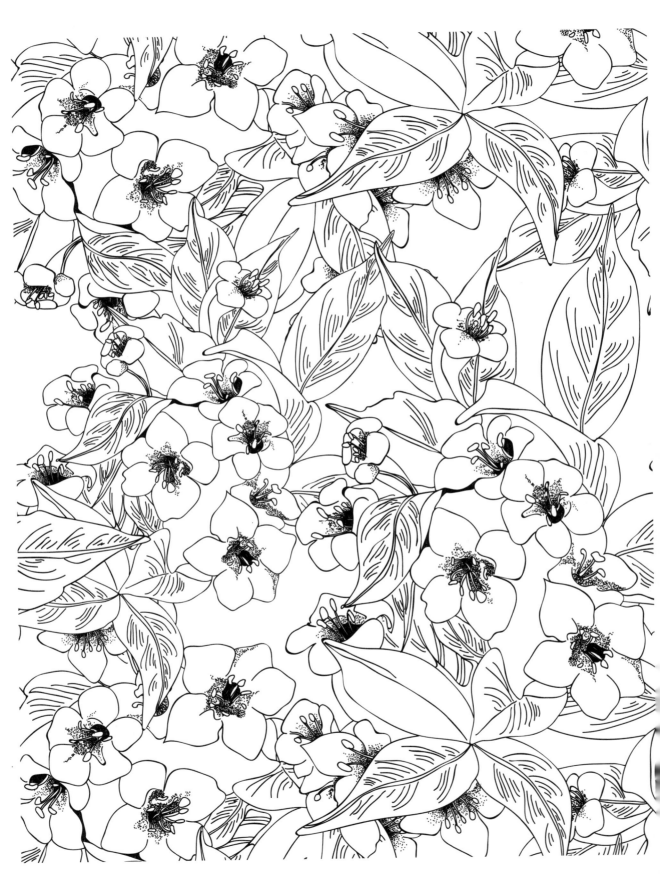

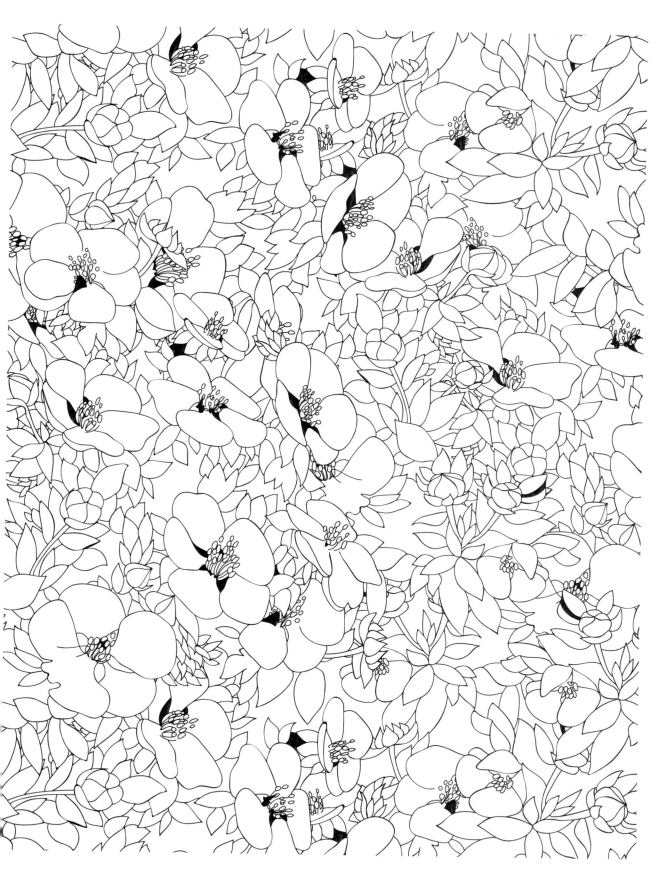

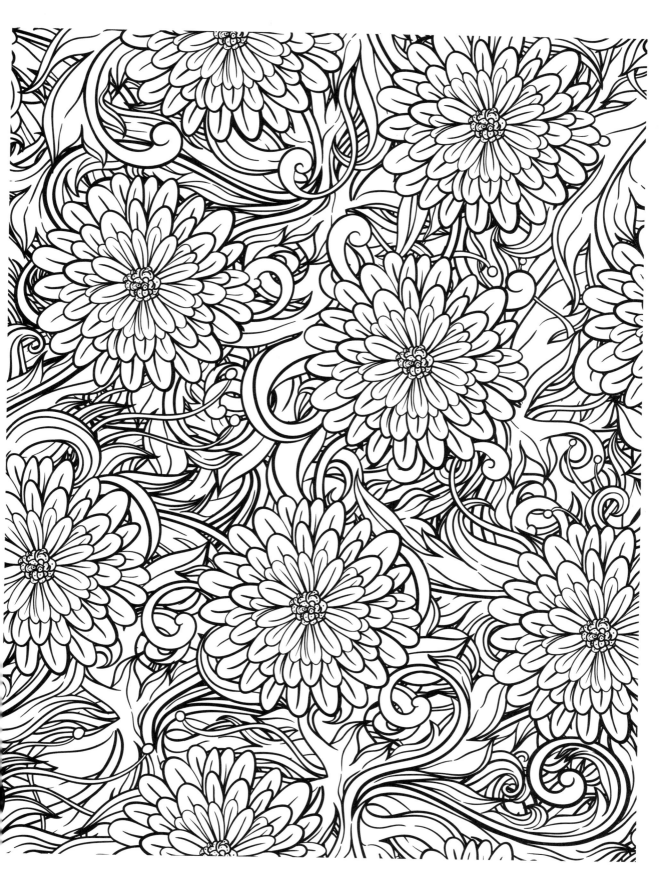

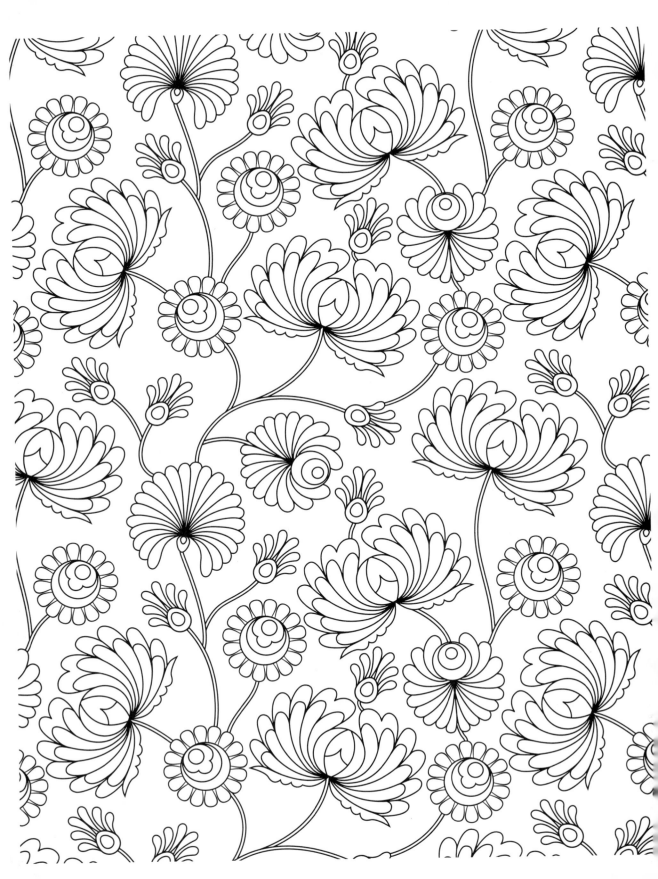

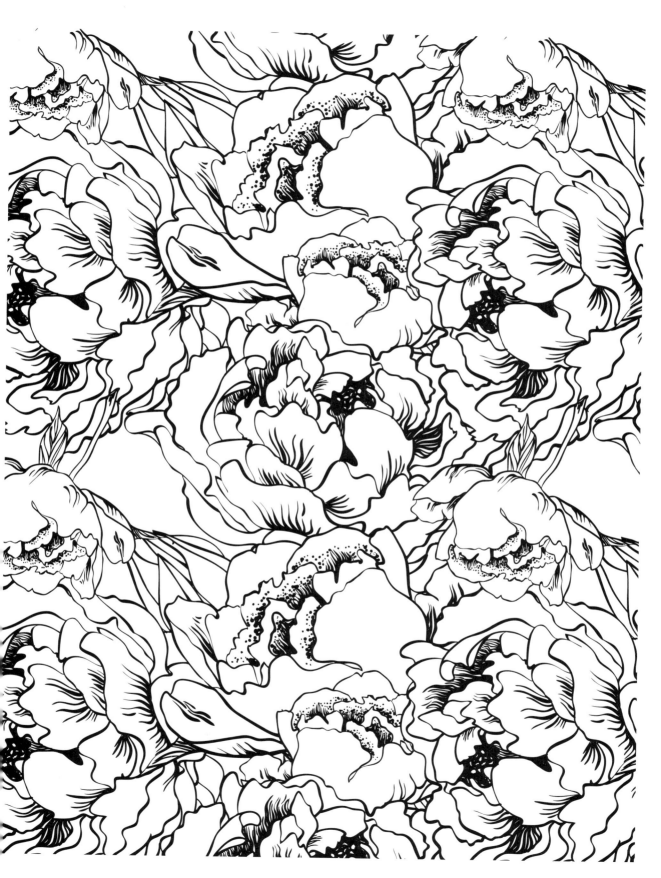

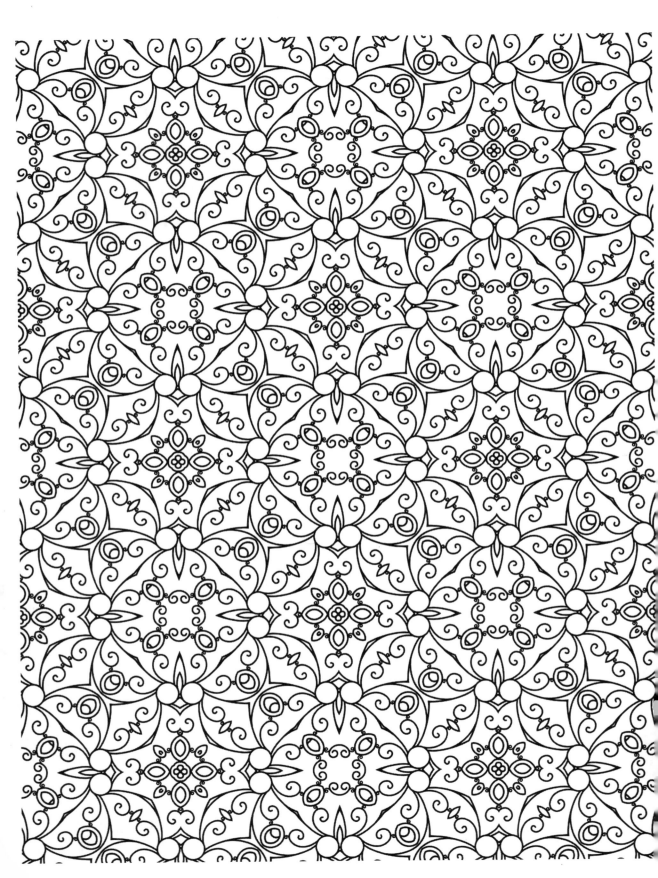

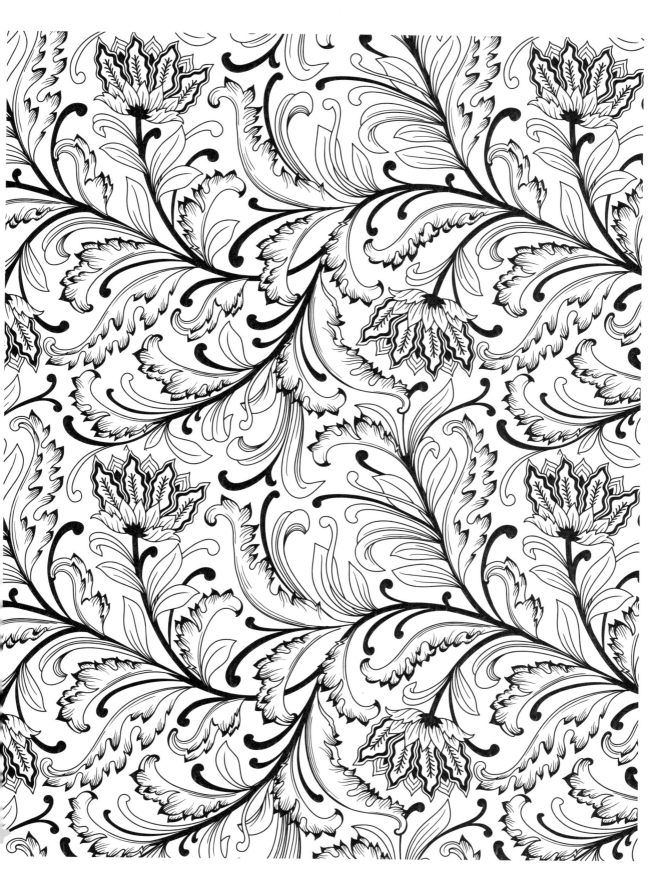